Lyndon Johnson and the Great Society

LYNDON JOHNSON AND THE GREAT SOCIETY

John A. Andrew III

The American Ways Series

IVAN R. DEE   *Chicago*

Library of Congress Cataloging-in-Publication Data:
Andrew, John A.
   Lyndon Johnson and the Great Society / John A. Andrew.
     p. cm. — (The American ways series)
   Includes bibliographical references and index.
   ISBN 1-56663-184-X (cloth : alk. paper). — ISBN 1-56663-185-8
(pbk. : alk. paper)
    1. United States—Politics and government—1963–1969.
2. Johnson, Lyndon B. (Lyndon Baines), 1908–1973. 3. United
States—Economic policy—1961–1971. 4. United States—Social
policy. 5. Social legislation—United States—History—20th
century. I. Title. II. Series.
E846.A62 1998
973.923—dc21   97-38966

For Roz

Contents

Acknowledgments   ix

Introduction   3
Defining characteristics of the Great Society. The tax cut. The
Johnson task forces. The 1964 election.

1 From Civil Rights to Race   23
The 1964 Civil Rights Act. The Voting Rights Act of 1965. The
Moynihan Report. Affirmative action and urban riots. Civil rights
moves north. The Civil Rights Act of 1968.

2 The War on Poverty   56
Social scientists and poverty. Johnson's alternative paths to combat
poverty. The debate over legislation. The Economic Opportunity
Act of 1964. Problems that undermined the war. Head Start. The
continuing debate over assessments of the war.

3 Health and Education   95
Debates over medical care for the aged. Legislation and problems. A
rising tide of criticism. Federal aid to education. Failures in the
Kennedy administration. Elementary and Secondary Education Act
of 1965. The interaction of education and race.

4 Model Cities   131
Urban renewal in the 1950s. The Housing and Urban Development
Act of 1965. The New Haven experience. Urban riots and Model
Cities. The problems of urban revival and the 1967 Detroit riot. The
Kerner Commission and the urban crisis in 1968. The Housing Act
of 1968. Weaknesses and criticisms of Model Cities.

5 Quality of Life   163
Consumer issues and Ralph Nader. Consumer protection legislation.
The business reaction. Beautification and the environment lead to
environmental protection efforts. The promotion of national
cultural life. Combating crime. The fading dream of a postscarcity
future.

6 Assessing the Great Society   183
    The Great Society as a liberal interlude. Changes since the 1960s.
    The influence of Great Society programs. Challenges to critics.

A Note on Sources   200

Index   208

Acknowledgments

HISTORIANS NEVER work alone. I want to thank John Braeman and Ivan Dee for proposing this book, and Lewis Gould for his constant encouragement. My interest in the Johnson presidency has grown steadily, both from teaching these years and finding a dearth of good classroom material and from my own research into the period.

The interlibrary loan office at Franklin & Marshall College worked diligently to acquire several volumes that proved useful in my research. My students in seminars and survey courses pushed me to complete this study through their constant befuddlement over aspects of the Great Society, along with their curiosity as to why it was so important. I hope they find answers in the pages that follow. David Schuyler and Lewis L. Gould graciously read the entire manuscript and offered cogent suggestions for improvement. John Braeman also gave the entire project thorough scrutiny and offered provocative comments. Any problems that remain, of course, are mine alone.

J. A. A.

Lancaster, Pennsylvania
January 1998

Lyndon Johnson and the Great Society

Introduction

ON NOVEMBER 10, 1994, almost thirty years to the day after Lyndon Johnson became the thirty-sixth president of the United States, Republican House leader Newt Gingrich declared that "profound things went wrong with the Great Society and the counterculture and until we address them head-on, we're going to have these problems." The next day, speaking before a Washington research group, the man who was about to become Speaker of the House attacked the Great Society as a "redistributionist model of how wealth is acquired," permeated by a "counterculture value system." Together they produced a "disaster." Even while he used Lyndon Johnson's words, urging his audience to support an "opportunity society," Gingrich blamed the Great Society for virtually every problem that had arisen during the intervening thirty years: poverty, welfare, public housing projects, unmet educational needs, government regulation, and higher taxes. He charged that the Great Society and the counterculture of the sixties shared a system of values, and concluded with a call to counterrevolution: "we have to say to the counterculture: nice try, you failed, you're wrong, and we have to simply, calmly, and methodically reassert American civilization. . . ."

Lyndon Johnson had once warned that the greatest danger to American stability was the "politics of principle"; but the attack on the Great Society by Gingrich and Republican conservatives in the 1980s and 1990s represented not only a difference of principle but an attempt to demonize the past and influence historical memory. The sixties have once again become contested territory. Conservatives stridently propagate their belief that a wayward liberalism moved to the left after 1964 and strayed from the values of mainstream America; liberals either reflexively defend the events and programs of that period or quietly mutter about "what went wrong." In their efforts to score political points with an increasingly apathetic electorate, both sides distort the past.

In this book I hope to redress those distortions. I focus on the underlying ideas and principal objectives of the original Great Society legislation, not on later amendments adopted during other (chiefly Republican) administrations, amendments that frequently transformed Great Society programs into something quite different from what was envisioned during the 1960s. The problems of liberalism since 1968 have obscured the earlier idealism that drove efforts to fulfill civil rights, attack poverty, address urban problems, provide medical care to the aged, deliver quality education to all children, and improve the quality of American life by curbing polluted air and water, enhancing the environment, or supporting the arts.

Because the problems that the Great Society sought to address were fundamental, not only to life in the United States but to the lives of its citizens, in any reconsideration readers need to keep in mind several questions. Did the Great Society test the limits of legislation to induce change? Can government really do anything significant to remedy pervasive social problems? Did expectations of change accelerate so rapidly during the 1960s that legislative machinery and government bureaucracy were unable to keep pace? Is mere reform sufficient? Or are the problems structural, requiring more fundamental changes? In short, is the American system basically sound except for the provision of help for the unfortunate, or is a more radical transformation needed? And was it possible to accomplish either within the context of Lyndon Johnson's consensus politics? Because the problems challenged in the 1960s remain largely unresolved even today, contemporary critics of the Great Society such as Newt Gingrich can plausibly use these problems to criticize the efforts of sixties liberals.

When Lyndon Johnson entered the White House in November 1963, the nation was preoccupied with other matters. The cold war had focused attention on enemies abroad, but in the wake of John F. Kennedy's assassination Americans' attention turned to the domestic arena. Mixed with expressions of shock, grief, and uncertainty was a concern over growing evidence of bitterness and hatred in American life. The American people had lost their innocence. LBJ quickly understood the essential need for unity, and he worked to forge consensus in nonstop behind-the-scenes meetings even while JFK lay in state.

The mood in the wake of Kennedy's assassination produced for LBJ a fortuitous interregnum. Johnson needed to establish himself as president and as leader. Yet even while he seized on the nation's grief, he had to battle the ghosts of the emerging myth of Camelot. His problems were largely personal: he was not John Kennedy, not urbane and sophisticated, not part of the Eastern establishment, and not liked or trusted either by liberals or their constituencies that formed the heart of the Democratic party. His reputation as a crass wheeler-dealer in the backrooms of politics, forged through years in the Senate, led liberals to suspect that he would sacrifice ideals for a deal.

More important, Johnson inherited a Congress in which conservatives of both parties had created a stalemate that stalled legislation. In the face of national needs, government seemed incapable of significant action. Kennedy's bills on poverty, medical care, and education appeared doomed. Neither of the two most active bills, on civil rights and a tax cut, were near passage. And on the eve of a presidential election year, prospects for action seemed slim.

Finally, a profound transformation was in process, as yet little understood: the United States was entering the media age. In the fall of 1963 the major networks had expanded their nightly news programs to thirty minutes. JFK had been perfect for television. In many respects he was America's first media hero as president. The Beatles were about to land in New York, creating their own media frenzy. Lyndon Johnson, however, did not fit well with this emerging medium. For all his skill at communicating with the Congress, he had great difficulty communicating with the American people through television. The animated politician on the stump or in the Senate cloakroom became a wooden, old-fashioned figure on the television screen. With civil rights tensions mounting steadily, and with the memory of John Kennedy looming larger in death than in life, the public hungered for public leadership. Lyndon Johnson would provide that leadership, but more often it would be behind the scenes than before the cameras. For the moment, however, that was not a liability; Johnson successfully wrapped himself in the mantle of his fallen predecessor. "Let us continue," he said, and with those words he set out not only to break the congressional logjam of legislation but to develop an extensive program of his own.

Several factors are central to understanding the issues of the Great Society and the era in which they emerged. One is the idealism that criticized the prevailing consensus and argued that Americans could do better. This predated the arrival of Lyndon Johnson in the White House and helps account for the Kennedy-era origins of many Great Society programs. Many Americans sought to cast aside what they saw as the social paralysis of the 1950s and redeem the promise of postwar affluence. Civil rights efforts led this rebirth of idealism, and demands for social change in the sixties consistently outpaced government efforts at reform. Ironically, by the time LBJ launched the Great Society in 1964, many of the foot soldiers pushing those demands, in SNCC (the Student Non-Violent Coordinating Committee) and SDS (Students for a Democratic Society) for example, had become cynical about prospects for reform. They had confronted the system and realized how resistant it was to change, even to mild reform, and had already moved on to more systemic critiques of existing economic, political, and social institutions and policies. But the middle class still believed in the transformative power of American ideals, even for the most intractable problems. And it was to the middle class that Johnson appealed for support.

Another defining characteristic of the Great Society was its backdrop of major social and cultural change. The late sixties was a time of intense polarization which inevitably spilled over into economic and political affairs. Disentangling Great Society reforms from the impact of the war in Vietnam, rising anti-Americanism at home and abroad, the counterculture, the emerging women's movement, and the broad challenge to traditional values was not possible. Here lay the roots of later controversy. As the Great Society sought to enlarge the consensus, critical movements for social and political change argued that too often the consensus was racist, sexist, or homophobic.

Several alternatives for change emerged in the late 1960s. One attacked the Great Society from the left, arguing for structural change to redistribute power as much as wealth. Without access to power, groups such as SDS and SNCC argued, people remained dispossessed. Another alternative came from the right, as Young Americans for Freedom and other conservatives embraced a free-market conservatism. They argued against government programs and government interference with the "natural order." Government should shrink, not grow, because big government inhibited rather than provided opportunity. A third position, a centrist one occupied by traditional liberals in the 1960s and epitomized by the Great Society, was that of managerial liberalism. President John F. Kennedy had best summarized its essence in a 1962 speech at Yale University. The current problems, he noted, "do not lend themselves to the great sort of 'passionate movements' which have stirred this country so often in the past. Now they deal with questions which are beyond the comprehension of most men, most governmental administrators, over which experts may differ, and yet we operate through our traditional political system." This cast government as the elite-dominated problem-solver, a perspective that fit well with Lyndon Johnson's predilections.

Like other liberals, Johnson believed the system was fundamentally sound but required mild reforms and technical adjustments so that it might provide opportunity for everyone. The government could balance the interests of various social and economic groups and sustain a consensus. Within liberal ranks, however, a division arose over what it meant to provide opportunity—ameliorative reform to alleviate the *symptoms* of distress, or structural change to eradicate the *causes* of pervasive problems? This confusion later became most evident in the Community Action Programs of the War on Poverty.

The Great Society eventually discovered the limits of consensus: it could be maintained only by avoiding divisive issues. But the issues addressed by Great Society programs were so important that they were bound to be divisive. The problem came with success, civil rights leader Vernon Jordan later observed, when privileged groups had to share their rights and privileges with the newly empowered. Stability and change did not go easily together. Conservative critics later commin-

gled the left and centrist positions in an effort to discredit the
Great Society, blaming the decade's race riots, social violence,
antiwar activities, and inflationary economics on LBJ's efforts
to redress inequities in American society.

Unlike the New Deal of the depression thirties, the Great
Society occurred amidst affluence. More important, perhaps,
was the popular assumption that this affluence had become a
permanent feature of the economic landscape and would continue indefinitely. This freed the middle class to focus on the
problems of others, supporting initiatives to extend opportunity to the less fortunate without fearing that their own opportunities would diminish. Managerial liberalism assumed
that government could fine-tune the economy to sustain economic growth, producing a growth dividend of surplus funds
to initiate reforms. The middle class could therefore embrace
change without fearing that they themselves would be
changed—or such was their perception. This was redemption
without sacrifice, the fulfillment of moral sensibilities without
personal pain. When this assumption changed and limits to
economic growth appeared, the public mood shifted.

Finally there is Lyndon Johnson, who had two presidencies:
the Great Society and the war in Vietnam. Although they cannot be totally divorced, this book focuses on the Great Society.
Not only was Johnson central to the vision of a Great Society,
his personality and political skills were crucial to the politics
necessary to implement it. As fellow Texan John B. Connally
observed, "There is no adjective in the dictionary to describe
him. He was cruel and kind, generous and greedy, sensitive
and insensitive, crafty and naive, ruthless and thoughtful, simple in many ways yet extremely complex, caring and totally
not caring . . . he knew how to use people in politics in the way
nobody else could that I know of." Johnson courted public ac-
claim and was highly sensitive to criticism. He was a man of

multiple personalities and mercurial moods—secretive, suspicious, a reservoir of enormous energy, unlimited ambition, and unrelenting paternalism. His biographer Paul Conkin called LBJ the "Big Daddy from the Pedernales." Reporter David Halberstam wrote that his "genes were seemingly larger and more demanding than those of other men; he dominated other men, leaning on them, sensing that every man had his price or his breaking point." Former Johnson aide Bill Moyers said simply, "Hyperbole was to Lyndon Johnson what oxygen is to life."

Johnson has been as elusive for historians to understand as he was for his contemporaries. But one can no more talk of the Great Society without Lyndon Johnson than one can recall the New Deal without Franklin Roosevelt. And this is no accident; Johnson wished to be remembered as a great president, to be spoken of in the same terms as his early hero, FDR. Warts and all, he embodied the essence of managerial liberalism. His own life—a childhood in the hardscrabble hills of central Texas, teaching poor children in south Texas, working for New Deal agencies, then a long career in the Congress— had indelibly shaped his conviction that government could be a positive force for change. He believed that the future was not predetermined, that public energies and resources could create opportunity where none existed.

Yet even as he was so much a part of the Great Society, LBJ seemed unable to comprehend the eddies and currents of social reform that swirled around him during the late sixties. He could never understand, for instance, why various minorities refused to recognize that he had their best interests at heart. Why wouldn't they let him "do good," not only *for* them but *to* them? Even as he sought stability and consensus, his own words bespoke a more turbulent social activism. "The Great Society," Johnson argued, "is not a safe harbor, a resting place, a final objective, a finished work. It is a challenge constantly renewed, beckoning us toward a destiny where the meaning of our lives matches the marvelous products of our labor." Was his vision plausible? Can a society adopt a broad reform agenda—inevitably affecting particular groups—maintaining a consensus?

Johnson certainly believed that it could, and when he defined his vision for the Great Society he painted a picture of harmonious change. But as Richard Goodwin worked over the text of LBJ's Great Society speech in May 1964, he noted that "the country was alive with change: ideas and anger, intellectual protest and physical rebellion. Without this ferment," Goodwin admitted, "the formulation of the Great Society would not have been possible, not even conceivable." Political scientist Hans Morgenthau concluded that "the Great Society and consensus cannot be had at the same time." To achieve the Great Society would mean social conflict, and Johnson would have to choose between consensus or his cherished vision. But the president did not see things that way; he believed to the end that both were possible. He did so, Morgenthau argued, because he confused consensus with the consent of the governed. In his memoirs Johnson himself said as much: "To me, consensus meant, first, deciding what needed to be done regardless of the political implications and, second, convincing a majority of the Congress and the American people of the necessity of doing those things."

Goodwin later wrote: "I believed that government, acting as the agent of a collective will, could change the circumstances of our daily life—our cities and environment, the quality of education, the restoration of 'power to the people.' " But, as Morgenthau hinted, could government change those "circumstances" without also altering the existing structure of American society? How would a top-down model of political

change mesh with growing grassroots desires for political empowerment? The answers can be found in the struggles to
control Great Society programs.

When Lyndon Johnson talked about his visions for the
Great Society, he used language that simultaneously emphasized the excitement and struggle of fundamental change
while seeming to ignore the possibility that some people might
not themselves wish to be changed. And LBJ vigorously embraced change as a positive value. To *Washington Post* reporter
Dorothy McCardle he depicted it as something other than
"the ordered, changeless and sterile battalion of the ants." For
him it was "the excitement of . . . always becoming, trying,
probing, falling, resting and trying again—but always trying
and always gaining." Always "gaining" meant never retreat-
ing, never losing. The battle was joined, but victory was assured. "If you wish a sheltered and uneventful life," Johnson
said at one point, "you are living in the wrong generation. No
one can promise you calm, or ease, or undisturbed comfort.
But we can promise you this—we can promise enormous
challenge and arduous struggle, hard labor, and great danger.
And with them we can promise you triumph over all the enemies of man."

On May 22, 1964, in a commencement address at the University of Michigan, the president expressed long-simmering
thoughts about a "Great Society." As he outlined his expansive
hopes, he acknowledged that they rested "on abundance and
liberty for all." If economic growth was sufficient to bring
prosperity to all, the United States now must address problems of poverty and racial injustice as well as obstacles to opportunity and a higher quality of life for all its citizens. As
Johnson described what must be done to build his Great Society, his sweep was all-inclusive. What escaped notice, however, was the experimental nature of the president's ideas. To

the graduates he admitted that "I do not pretend that we have the full answer to those problems. But I do promise this: We are going to assemble the best thought and the broadest knowledge from all over the world to find those answers for America." In words that seem ironic with hindsight, he cautioned that the "solution to these problems does not rest on a massive program in Washington. . . . They require . . . a creative federalism. . . ." He closed with a series of challenges to the graduates. This was to be a spiritual and moral crusade, and the transformative power was in their hands. They were Americans, and they could accomplish anything they set their sights on. With an unblinking assertion that this was still the American Century, the president proclaimed that "we have the power to shape the civilization that we want." The details would come later.

When they did they were impressive. By the time the Eighty-ninth Congress adjourned in October 1966, LBJ had asked for 200 major pieces of legislation; Congress had approved 181 of them. In itself this tidal wave of new laws transformed the role of the federal government in the lives of most Americans. The president's sweeping proposals sought to remedy almost every ill that was thought to afflict Americans or their nation: civil rights, poverty, education, health, housing, pollution, the arts, cities, occupational safety, consumer protection, and mass transit, to name only the most prominent. LBJ adopted programs, his aide Joseph Califano later noted, "the way a child eats rich chocolate-chip cookies."

Aware that his program was premised on continued economic prosperity, LBJ believed that it reflected a broad consensus. Speaking to an audience in Detroit in late June 1964, the president proclaimed that "We stand at the edge of the greatest era in the life of any nation. For the first time in world history, we have the abundance and the ability to free every man from hopeless want. . . . This nation . . . has man's first chance to create a Great Society. . . ." The programs would intrude on the lives of most Americans, but since they demanded little in the way of personal sacrifice, they would not be intrusive. The "essential concept of the Great Society," Pennsylvania Senator Joseph Clark, a liberal Democrat, observed, was "that America possesses the resources, properly marshaled and directed by social purpose, to rid our civilization of the ills that have plagued mankind from the beginning of time."

To secure and perpetuate the base of prosperity that generated those resources, the president grounded much of his plans on a tax cut. Already proposed by President Kennedy before his assassination, it promised to increase federal revenues dramatically and fund the Great Society. As it turned out, the war in Vietnam would siphon off those additional funds and more. But as the White House planned the 1964 tax cut it was wildly optimistic that the reduction would generate a robust growth dividend: economic advisers projected a $35 billion increase in federal revenues by 1970. They had good reason for their optimism. Between 1960 and 1965 corporate profits rose 52 percent before taxes and 67 percent after taxes. Even the take-home pay of factory workers rose by 21 percent (13 percent in real dollars). The consumer price index, by contrast, rose an average of only 1.3 percent annually between 1961 and 1965. In other words, in the absence of significant inflation, growth was largely real. The 1964 tax cut sought to stimulate production still further, thus producing major increases in the gross national product, creating jobs, and enhancing disposable personal income and corporate profits.

Kennedy's tax bill had gone to Congress in late January

1963. It linked tax-rate reductions with tax reform to close loopholes. But Chairman Wilbur Mills of the House Ways and Means Committee heeded the cries of lobbyists and opposed the reforms. By fall only the cuts remained, and few individuals could be found who opposed tax cuts. The bill passed early the next year, and LBJ signed it on February 26, 1964. It cut taxes by $10 billion over the next two years. Individual tax-rate scales fell from 20 to 91 percent (1963), to 16 to 77 percent (1964), to 14 to 70 percent (1965). Individual withholding rates fell too, and corporate tax rates declined from 52 percent in 1963 to 48 percent in 1965. By 1967 federal revenues climbed dramatically to $150 billion, compared with $94 billion in 1961. The GNP soared by more than 10 percent in the year following passage of the tax bill, and disposable personal income rose by 15 percent in 1966. Employment kept pace, and the number of jobless declined by almost one million during the next two years. By December 1965 the unemployment rate was only 4.1 percent; in January 1966 it fell to 3.9 percent. Economic growth averaged 4.5 percent per year from 1961 to 1968 (although in the late 1960s some of this growth came from spending on Great Society programs and the war in Vietnam). In the four years following passage of the tax cut, nonfinancial corporations enjoyed an average after-tax rate of return of 9 percent—the highest in two decades.

With the tax cut securing future economic prosperity, LBJ believed that both the public and business sectors would realize they could afford to fund social programs. Indeed, the president saw the Great Society as the final link in the transformation of liberalism from the social democratic reform impulses of the early 1930s to the managerial liberalism of the 1960s. The key to that transformation was economic growth. What LBJ hoped to do with the Great Society was to use that growth to fund social programs to aid those who had been by-passed by affluence.

To generate ideas, Johnson made extensive use of special task forces. Throughout 1964 and after, he gathered groups of scholars and experts to develop public policy alternatives. "I want to get the advice of the best brains in the country on the problems and challenges confronting America," the president said, "and I want their help in devising the best approach to meeting them. I want these task forces to question what we now are doing and to suggest better ways of doing it. . . . Let's set our sights too high rather than too low."

By the fall of 1964 more than fourteen such task forces had created a legislative agenda to implement the initial promises of the Great Society. They worked in secret—LBJ treasured secrecy—under the supervision of Johnson aide Bill Moyers, and represented, as the historian Hugh Davis Graham has noted, an innovation in the formulation of presidential policy. They fulfilled the promise Johnson made to Michigan graduates, to assemble the "best thought and broadest knowledge from all over the world." They produced a cornucopia of legislation. After the success of the early task forces, additional groups formed under the guidance of Joseph Califano to provide systematic recommendations for legislation that the president might include in his annual State of the Union Message. Perhaps more than any other aspect of the Great Society planning, the Johnson task forces illustrated the core ideology of managerial liberalism. They used intellectual and technological experts to analyze problems and propose solutions to public problems, and rested on a faith that government then had only to provide sufficient resources to resolve the problem. The experts were to create the programs, the politicians were to pass them, the bureaucrats were to administer them. The electorate would be the beneficiaries of this missionary zeal.

But this top-down elitist approach to public policy meant that legislative proposals did not necessarily carry with them an active or natural constituency beyond the experts, politicians, and bureaucrats who were central to their creation. It led to an image of the Great Society as an alien or imperious bureaucratic monster. LBJ sought to create a national community, but local communities did not wish to be homogenized in some great national blender whose switch was controlled from the White House.

Other problems loomed. One was Vietnam. Only thirteen months after the tax cut, U.S. ground combat troops arrived in Vietnam to initiate a new, much more costly phase in that conflict. In the short term LBJ swept aside the concerns of Vietnam through secrecy, devious rhetoric, and fraudulent budget projections for the conduct of the war. Another problem was even less apparent, and its impact has drawn much less attention than the war in Vietnam. This was the onrushing demographic phenomenon known as the baby-boom generation. In 1964 the leading edge of that generation turned eighteen and began entering the job market. Almost two and a half times more Americans would enter the labor force between 1965 and 1980 than between 1950 and 1965. The implications of this glut were frightening, though there is little evidence that White House advisers thought much about them. One analyst has called this the "crowded generation"—a population larger than the entire labor force of France or West Germany was entering the American labor market. Whatever expectations Lyndon Johnson or anyone else held for the Great Society, this demographic explosion threatened their best efforts by overburdening job markets as well as virtually all other aspects of American social and economic life.

Understanding the well-intended psychology that fueled the creation of the Great Society is essential to understanding the controversy that later surrounded alternative approaches to problem-solving, such as community action or "maximum feasible participation of the poor." The Great Society's potential rested, as did so much else, on Lyndon Johnson's conception of the consensus. This meant, in brief, that LBJ's task forces would deal with clearly identifiable problems broadly recognized by the general public and propose solutions before the problems themselves became divisive political issues. That is why the 1964 presidential election provided an important ingredient for the Great Society.

The campaign of Barry Goldwater in 1964 had begun after the 1960 Republican convention in Chicago, when party conservatives recoiled in horror at Richard Nixon's appeasement of New York Governor Nelson Rockefeller and the liberal wing of the party. Long dissatisfied with the "modern Republicanism" of Dwight Eisenhower, conservatives had hoped that one of their own might join Nixon on the 1960 ticket. They failed, and after that failure retreated to various encampments to plan a takeover of the party. Anticipating Goldwater's nomination, they looked forward to an ideological contest with John Kennedy in which Goldwater would break through in the solidly Democratic South by offering "a choice, not an echo." But with Kennedy's assassination in November 1963, Lyndon Johnson, a Southerner, became the Democratic president. Even at that early date, many of the leaders of the conservative cause knew their candidate was doomed; Goldwater himself admitted as much. But the rank-and-file faithful remained true believers, and conservatives such as William Rusher and William F. Buckley, Jr., of the *National Review* argued that the real stakes in 1964 involved the future direction of the Republican party. They kept the faith.

But their candidate, not their conservative ideology, became the central focus of the campaign. When he accepted the Re-

publican nomination, Goldwater did so with the ringing declaration that "Extremism in the defense of liberty is no
vice. . . . Moderation in the pursuit of justice is no virtue."
Then, as he campaigned across the country, his every speech
seemed to alienate more voters. Like the press, even many Republicans viewed Goldwater as a radical extremist and
flocked to the Johnson camp.

The election returns told the story. The Johnson-Hum-
phrey ticket amassed 43,126,218 votes to 27,174,898
for Goldwater-Miller, winning 61 percent of the nearly
71 million voters who went to the polls. Republicans carried
only six states: Arizona, Alabama, Georgia, Louisiana, Mississippi, and South Carolina. In addition, Goldwater's coat-
tails dragged many prominent Republicans—such as Senate
candidates Charles Percy in Illinois and Robert Taft, Jr.,
in Ohio—down to defeat. In the Congress, 28 Democratic
senators and 295 Democratic representatives were elected,
giving the Democrats a 68-to-32 margin in the Senate, and
a 295-to-140 dominance in the House. Many of the Democratic victories occurred in normally Republican districts and
would likely revert to traditional voting patterns at the next
election, so Johnson knew that his "mandate" was limited. It
was, he told friends, like the Rio Grande—broad but not
deep.

The 1964 elections so eviscerated Republican strength in
Congress that there was little likelihood of divisive debates
over key Great Society measures. Four days before the election, knowing that victory was assured, Lyndon Johnson had
spoken to an enthusiastic throng in New York's Madison
Square Garden. What he said there was not a startling depar-
ture from his earlier speeches about his visions for a Great Society. What was significant about his words, however, was
their very lack of specificity.

This nation, this people, this generation, has man's first opportunity to create the Great Society. It can be a society of success without squalor, beauty without barrenness, works of genius without the wretchedness of poverty. We can open the doors of learning, of fruitful labor and rewarding leisure, not just to the privileged few, but we can open them to everyone. These goals cannot be measured by the size of our bank balance. They can only be measured in the quality of the lives our people lead. Millions of Americans have achieved prosperity, and they have found prosperity alone is just not enough. They need a chance to seek knowledge and to touch beauty, to rejoice in achievement and in the closeness of family and community.

The weakness of the opposition in 1964 led Lyndon Johnson to overestimate the breadth and perhaps the very nature of the consensus. Election results gave the president a victory that exceeded the basic convictions and commitment of the American public to sweeping reform. The moderate middle of the electorate had no place to go but to LBJ. It remained to be seen whether they had given him their vote or their commitment. Immediately neither seemed to be a problem. For a two-year period at least, the election dramatically altered the political alignment in Congress and created a liberal majority for the first time since the early 1930s. To party goers at his inaugural ball the president advised, "Don't stay up too late. We're on our way to the Great Society." He told his aide Larry O'Brien, "We can pass it all now."

That proved to be true, but buried in the election results were seeds of longer-term changes in the electorate. Goldwater had narrowly carried the popular vote in the South, 49 to 48.9 percent, and Johnson had lost a majority of the white vote throughout the region, except in his home state of Texas. In the four Southern states that Goldwater carried, he did so by amassing an overwhelming percentage of the white vote: 87 percent in Mississippi, 69.5 percent in Alabama, 57 percent in South Carolina and Louisiana, and 54 percent in Georgia. At least two Southern states, Georgia and Mississippi, had elected their first Republican congressmen in the twentieth century. What these changes meant was still unclear. But at the very least they forecast that Johnson's efforts during the campaign to avoid specifics and make Barry Goldwater the chief issue, as well as his use of secret task forces to mask discussion of the most prominent issues, were not entirely successful in soothing parts of the traditional Democratic constituency.

For the time being LBJ, though, had his liberal majority. Convinced that the first year was the best time to strike, he launched a full-scale offensive to create the Great Society. To ease the way, Democrats used their new liberal majority to alter the House rules. First they circumvented the Rules Committee bottleneck, which conservative Southern Democrats had traditionally used to block legislation, by giving committee chairmen the authority to call for a floor vote any measure that the Rules Committee had held for twenty-one days. Once the measure was on the floor, the majority could then work its will. The Democratic majority also eliminated the delaying tactics of individual House members. They could no longer object to a reconciliation conference with the Senate on legislation that had passed the two houses in slightly different form, nor could they delay the consideration of legislation by requesting a certified copy of the bill. Democrats also enforced party discipline, stripping two Southern Democrats—John Bell Williams of Mississippi and Albert Watson of South Carolina—of their seniority because they had supported Barry Goldwater in the 1964 campaign. Finally they altered the party membership of all committees to reflect the new Democratic majorities in the House. This further weakened the power of conservatives to obstruct legislation at the committee level.

When Lyndon Johnson delivered his State of the Union Message on January 4, 1965, to the opening session of the Eighty-ninth Congress, he warned that "We are only at the beginning of the road to the Great Society." He then proposed a sweeping series of measures to combat disease, urban blight, air and water pollution, regional economic decline, denial of voting rights, neglect of the arts, and waste in government. Johnson meant to move, and move fast. As he told the National Urban League in December 1964: "Great social change tends to come rapidly in periods of intense activity before the impulse slows. I believe we are in the midst of such a period of change. Now, the lights are still on in the White House tonight—preparing programs that will keep our country up with the times."

But what the president styled as "the beginning" actually rested on two legislative initiatives left over from the Kennedy years. They had already been enacted into law, though the implications of neither was yet clear—civil rights and poverty. These issues lay at the heart of Lyndon Johnson's dreams for a Great Society and revealed the fragile nature of his consensus. While the formative legislation in each case became law in 1964, before the election, both the issues and the legislation remained controversial and perpetually unfinished for the remainder of LBJ's term in office. When he left the White House in January 1969, neither issue had stabilized. Indeed, each was more troubling and inflammatory than when Johnson inherited the presidency. Together they represent the two great issues that beckoned Americans to the Great Society.

1

From Civil Rights to Race

ON NOVEMBER 27, 1963, five days after the assassination of President Kennedy, Lyndon Johnson spoke to a joint session of Congress and to the nation. While his larger purpose was to emphasize his theme of "Let us continue" the slain president's programs, he also used the occasion to rally support for passage of new civil rights legislation:

> No memorial oration or eulogy could more eloquently honor President Kennedy's memory than the earliest possible passage of the civil rights bills for which he fought so long. We have talked long enough in this country about equal rights. We have talked for one hundred years or more. It is now time to write the next chapter—and to write it in the books of law.

The 1964 Civil Rights Act, which had begun as the 1963 Civil Rights Bill but failed to move through the Congress before that dreadful day in Dallas, was a cornerstone of Lyndon Johnson's vision for the Great Society. The act sought to redeem the moral promise of the American Dream. By 1966, however, the unifying moral vision of civil rights had become a divisive nightmare of race. That journey from civil rights to race proved to be a landmark of change in the decade. It also marked a watershed for the Great Society.

By 1964 the need for new civil rights legislation was obvious to all but the most dedicated race baiter. In eleven key Southern states, school desegregation had barely advanced since 1960. Indeed, since 1954 the "all deliberate speed" of the Supreme Court's *Brown* decision had essentially meant no movement at all. By the 1963–1964 school year, only 1.2 percent of black children were attending school with white children in states of the former Confederacy. The promise of *Brown* had become a mockery of justice. In the aftermath of the 1963 March on Washington, the Gallup Poll revealed that less than a third of all Americans believed the federal government was pushing civil rights too fast.

The March on Washington had capped three years of sit-ins and other nonviolent direct-action protests which had seized the moral high ground for civil rights. These protests drew their sustenance primarily from black churches and communities throughout the South as well as from student and religious activists in the North. Civil rights was, in other words, a political movement driven by a constituency either outside of or largely peripheral to the existing political structure. But despite their efforts, and perhaps because of Southern whites' use of police dogs and fire hoses to forestall desegregation, by the fall of 1963 there had been little visible change. The frustration and disappointment of many civil rights activists had been evident during the March on Washington that August. John Lewis of SNCC had prepared a strident speech critical of the Kennedy administration's lack of movement, and had only reluctantly agreed to temper his remarks at the last moment. Even then, Lewis was angry and direct. "Where is the political party that will make it unnecessary to march on Washington?" he asked. "Where is the political party that will make it unnecessary to march in the streets of Birmingham?" "I want to know," he demanded, "which side is the Federal Government on?"

Despite broad Northern support for civil rights, so evident at the March on Washington, only marches and bombings in Birmingham, Alabama, and naked police brutality under the direction of Birmingham police commissioner Eugene "Bull" Connor, moved President Kennedy to back new civil rights legislation. By late November the administration's bill languished in committee. Kennedy's assassination, together with Lyndon Johnson's determination that nothing else would come to the Senate floor until the bill was passed, pushed the Civil Rights Bill of 1964 through the Congress.

The House passed the bill rather quickly, though the debate was occasionally sharp. Louisiana Representative Edwin Willis epitomized the Southern Democratic opposition, insisting that the bill "would cause strife and chaos among our people.... It will be resisted and contribute to violence in every State of this Union wherein the Federal Government intervenes under the various sections of the act." Armistead Selden, Jr., of Alabama cautioned that the bill contained "the seeds of an American totalitarianism." It was "legislation by duress and intimidation." But, as O. C. Fisher of Texas admitted, the votes were there to pass it in the House. "This is the de luxe model of the steamroller's advent into the decade of the sixties," he complained. "It is well lubricated, and it is on the move." Fisher predicted, however, that darker days lay ahead.

> One of these days some of the white folks may get tired of this sort of carrying on. One of these days the white folks may decide they have taken enough. And that warning applies to both parties to this coalition. These white folks may decide they need somebody to speak up for their rights— that is, what is left of their rights after the politicians get through carving them up.

But on February 7, 1964, Congressman Thomas Gill (Democrat, Hawaii) concluded that "time and tide wait for none of us. The tide of history has run on this question. The time is now." Three days later the House passed H.R. 7152 by a vote of 290 to 130.

The Senate battle for civil rights legislation in 1964, on the other hand, was titanic. Senate debate consumed more than eighty days and thousands of pages in the *Congressional Record*. Opposition to the bill produced the longest filibuster on record. Southern Democrats, led by Richard Russell of Georgia, mobilized to delay the bill. To counteract their efforts, Hubert Humphrey (Democrat, Minnesota) and California Republican Thomas Kuchel marshaled support for the legislation. Both sides believed that Republican Senator Everett Dirksen of Illinois held the key to its passage. Known as the "Wizard of Ooze," a man who "marinated his tonsils daily with a mixture of Pond's cold cream and water, which he gargled and swallowed," Dirksen was a conservative Midwesterner, and Midwestern Republicans held the balance of power in the Senate, poised between Southern Democrats who opposed civil rights and its liberal supporters in both parties. Democrats gave him the chance to embrace the bill as a Republican measure by adding some amendments, which he did. He endorsed the Equal Employment Opportunity Commission as a device to limit Justice Department intervention, provided for local agencies to handle job discrimination complaints before calling in the federal government, and limited the cutoff of federal funds to affected school districts and not to entire states. Dirksen was also a keen student of public opinion; by February 1964 he could see Gallup Poll figures showing that 61 percent of the public favored passage of the bill.

Southern Democrats resisted every step of the way with a

chorus of criticism. John Stennis of Mississippi warned that the "blessings of eternal and universal brotherhood are a beautiful ideal and a worthy objective, but if they cannot be obtained in the natural process of human behavior they cannot be obtained by the forces of law." His colleague James Eastland (whom *Time* magazine had labeled "the nation's most dangerous demagogue") was blunter, insisting that "segregation is not discrimination." It was a "social factor," whereas discrimination was an "economic factor." Sam Ervin of North Carolina charged that it was a "thought-control bill" because discrimination was a mental process. Other opponents, such as Texas Republican John Tower, attacked the bill as an unwarranted extension of federal power. It violated the constitutional "prerogatives of all Americans to live their own private lives and to conduct their own private businesses in accordance with their own individual wishes and desires."

Senator Russell Long of Louisiana turned the debate from civil rights to race. "It seems to me," he argued, "that every man of white Caucasian heritage has a perfect right to protect those institutions in his society which allow him the freedom to associate with people of his own race...." Legal scholar Robert Bork charged that the bill would "compel association even where it is not desired." Senator Richard Russell warned that the bill would "turn our social order upside down. It would have a tremendous impact on what we have called, in happier times, the American way of life."

To counter these attacks, supporters seized the moral high ground. There was a "seething restlessness" in the country, Edmund Muskie of Maine warned, and rhetoric would no longer soothe that impatience. Republican Jacob Javits of New York insisted that the bill represented more than another piece of legislation; it was a "struggle for the soul of the Nation." The bill's floor general, Hubert Humphrey, agreed.

"The question is," Humphrey asked his colleagues, "are we going to decide the issue with due process of law, or will it be decided in the streets and back alleys with clubs and violence?" Passing the civil rights act would, he hoped, take the issue "off the streets and put it into the legislative assembly and into the courts." That was unlikely; direct-action protest had been too successful and had mobilized too many hopes. But the sentiment appealed to Humphrey's fellow senators.

As the bill's opponents filibustered throughout the spring, its supporters quietly worked to secure Dirksen's support. Driven by his ego as well as by a conviction that the times demanded such legislation, Dirksen threw his support behind it. On June 9, 1964, West Virginia Democrat Robert Byrd, a former member of the Ku Klux Klan, opened a last-ditch effort to block the bill when he began an 800-page speech against cloture. The next day, more than 534 hours after it had begun, the filibuster ended. The 1964 Civil Rights Act, technically the Mansfield-Dirksen-Humphrey-Kuchel amendment, passed 73 to 27. The House quickly concurred to the amendment, 289 to 126.

Like many Southerners, Senator Strom Thurmond of South Carolina was bitter in defeat.

> This is a tragic day for America, when Negro agitators, spurred on by communist enticements to promote racial strife, can cause the United States Senate to be steamrollered into passing the worst, most unreasonable and unconstitutional legislation that has ever been considered by the Congress. This legislation will make a Czar of the President of the United States and a Rasputin of the Attorney General.

Governor George Wallace of Alabama was more defiant: "We must destroy the power to dictate, to forbid, to require, to demand, to distribute, to edict." The bill, which he labeled a "fraud, a sham and a hoax," would "live in infamy."

As passed, the Civil Rights Act of 1964 was a comprehensive bill that contained eleven sections or titles. The most significant were Titles I, II, VI, and VII. Title I expanded the right to vote by making the successful completion of the sixth grade *prima facie* evidence of literacy in order to qualify to vote in federal elections. Title II, which lay at the core of the bill, guaranteed access to public accommodations without regard to race, color, religion, or national origin. This was probably the most significant legislation for racial equality since the Fourteenth Amendment to the Constitution in 1868, and struck at the heart of the Southern social structure. It affected motels (if they had more than five rooms), restaurants, theaters, stadiums, and other public facilities. It spoke to the demands of Freedom Rides and sit-ins, and through the Constitution's commerce clause injected the federal government into the center of the struggle for civil rights.

Other sections of the bill enlarged that responsibility. Title VI banned racial discrimination in any program that received federal assistance. Noncompliance would cause the withholding of funds. This promised to be an effective countermeasure to Southern resistance to integration, especially after the passage of subsequent Great Society legislation, although in future years that promise was not always fulfilled. Title VII required equality of opportunity in employment and created the Equal Employment Opportunity Commission (EEOC) to replace a similar commission created by executive order under President Kennedy. In addition to banning discrimination on the basis of race, religion, or national origin, Congress also added the word "sex" to this title. Later, beginning in the 1970s, the women's movement would use this language to attack sex discrimination in the workplace and elsewhere. Congress, however, stripped out of this section authority for the EEOC to issue "cease and desist" orders, thereby forcing individuals to go to court to defend their rights in instances where discriminatory behavior persisted. Other titles enabled the federal government to initiate lawsuits to prevent discrimination in various ways. Title V extended the life of the Commission on Civil Rights, which had effectively publicized violations of civil rights throughout the South.

Passage of the 1964 Civil Rights Act solidified liberal support for the new president. It also brought LBJ the black vote in the 1964 election. In some urban precincts African-American support for the president reached 99 percent. In the short run, at least, the bill did not hurt Democrats among white voters (except in the South). There was simply no real alternative for them in 1964, and civil rights remained essentially a Southern issue. The real political key, perhaps, was the bill's impact among Southern civil rights advocates. And here the results were more complex. Where the president and Congress saw the bill as landmark legislation, civil rights activists and their constituents viewed it quite differently. For them it was only a beginning. It defined and protected rights already guaranteed in the Constitution and Bill of Rights, nothing more. It represented a step forward, but it was a small step and one long delayed.

Civil rights supporters had several other concerns. Would the legislation be enforced? The historical record was not encouraging, and Southern opposition remained unrepentant. Advocates determined to test the law at every opportunity. What would it take to enforce the provisions of the legislation? Title IV, for instance, specified that desegregation did not "mean the assignment of students to public schools in order to overcome racial imbalance." But what if other remedies failed to work? In 1971 the Supreme Court would endorse widespread busing as a proper corrective to racial discrimination. But in 1964 most Americans, or at least most white Northerners, remained optimistic that the nation's moral conscience would assert itself, convinced that the United States was a nation of laws. Voluntary compliance remained the goal, even in the face of such revolutionary change.

What lesson would be drawn from passage of the bill? Here civil rights activists paradoxically agreed with Southern segregationists: passage stemmed as much from insistent demonstrations as from other factors. The lesson, therefore, was clear: not only were more demonstrations needed to extend the umbrella of racial equality, they were likely to be effective in stimulating further legislation. Rather than dampen demonstrations, as Hubert Humphrey had hoped, the Civil Rights Act of 1964 promised to encourage them. Finally, what would be its political impact? Just after signing the bill LBJ told aide Bill Moyers, "I think we delivered the South to the Republican Party for your lifetime and mine." Would the act set in motion a political realignment in the country? And if it did, what were its implications?

The 1964 presidential election certainly proved nothing. Barry Goldwater had voted against the Civil Rights Act of 1964. Even though he did so because he embraced the principle of small government, and although his personal record was clearly one of nondiscrimination, his vote became symbolically significant. Like so much else that he said or did during the campaign, it demonstrated to voters that he was the wrong man for the job and that he fundamentally misunderstood the times. In addition, as the Goldwater campaign attracted—indeed courted—Southern segregationists and various groups from the right-wing fringe (such as the John Birch Society), it ceded not only the left but the center to Lyndon Johnson and the Democrats. The election propelled a new class of moderate and liberal Democrats into office. When the new Congress convened in January 1965, liberals enjoyed a clear majority for the first time since the mid-1930s.

Lyndon Johnson, not surprisingly, claimed a mandate. But at best LBJ's victory was a mandate to address some of the pressing issues that threatened the national consensus. It did not define those issues. Indeed, one could read the election as a ratification that the administration had done just that in passing the Civil Rights Act. Even LBJ understood the fragility of the liberal majority. The election destroyed neither conservatives nor Republicans; both would be back.

The campaign and election had nonetheless demonstrated two dangers for Johnson and the Democratic party. The first surfaced with the emergence of the Mississippi Freedom Democratic Party (MFDP) and its challenge to the regular (segregated) Mississippi delegation at the 1964 Democratic National Convention in Atlantic City. The MFDP had formed in April 1964, during the Southern filibuster of the civil rights bill, at a meeting in Jackson, Mississippi. It represented not only a challenge to the regular Democratic party in Mississippi but a conviction that the existing political system could still respond to change through grass-roots organizing and moral rectitude. Freedom Summer 1964 called national attention to racial problems within the state. In particular, the murder of three civil rights workers focused media attention on violence and inequality in Mississippi, escalating calls for change. When summer came, MFDP delegates climbed on buses and headed to Atlantic City, convinced that they would not only be heard by the convention's credentials committee but that their case was morally and politically sound. They *would* be seated.

Lyndon Johnson, however, would have none of it. Afraid

not only that the white Mississippi delegates would bolt the convention but that other Southern delegations would join them, the president ordered Hubert Humphrey—if Humphrey wanted the vice-presidency—to convince the MFDP delegates to accept two at-large seats, with a promise that their grievances would be addressed before the 1968 convention. Together with his able lieutenant, Walter Mondale, Humphrey did Johnson's bidding. Led by Fannie Lou Hamer, the MFDP delegates refused to budge. Hamer told the credentials committee how she had been arrested and beaten in Mississippi. Her ordeals were so moving and poignant that Johnson hastily called a news conference to preempt her televised testimony and preclude a rush of popular sentiment to the MFDP. Speaking for the other delegates, Hamer informed reporters, "We didn't come all this way for no two seats!" In the end Johnson preserved outward peace, but the MFDP delegates left Atlantic City disenchanted with the Democratic party and convinced that the system really did not mean to accommodate them. Liberalism had failed in their eyes, and younger activists turned to more radical solutions for systemic change.

The second danger was that even though Lyndon Johnson trounced Barry Goldwater in the national election, he lost the Southern vote to Goldwater. Where LBJ did win, he did so because of black voters. This not only portended a political realignment, as white Democratic voters moved into the Republican column, it also meant that Democrats needed black votes in the South if they were to retain control of presidential politics in the region.

Symbolic of this shift was the election of John Tower to Johnson's Texas Senate seat. Tower was the first Republican member of the Senate from the South since Reconstruction. Two weeks after the November election, accordingly, Louis

Martin of the Democratic National Committee outlined "Operation Dixie, 1964–65." This entailed not only black voter registration in those states that Goldwater carried but new voter-registration legislation. By January LBJ had endorsed the proposal, telling Acting Attorney General Nicholas Katzenbach to "write the goddamndest, toughest voting rights bill that you can devise." Party politics, perhaps more than civil rights, called the shots.

The problem was clear. Almost half of all Southern blacks were still disfranchised. In more than a hundred counties in the Deep South, less than 25 percent of the eligible black population was registered to vote. Although the Justice Department had filed sixty-seven voting rights suits the previous year, only sixteen had come to trial. Even the federal courts in the South were not reliable allies. How to move a voting rights bill through the Congress became the question. The president told Martin Luther King, Jr., that despite lopsided Democratic majorities he could not "get a voting rights bill through in this next session of Congress." To push such legislation, Johnson added, would endanger other pieces of his Great Society that needed Southern votes to pass, and the president preferred to focus on the War on Poverty and other social issues. King concluded that the civil rights movement had to return to the streets to create a climate of opinion that demanded such legislation as a moral corrective to flagrant violations of the fundamental right to vote. Since polls indicated that 95 percent of the public already believed a voting rights bill should be passed, King's objective was to force the hand of the president and Congress.

King and the Southern Christian Leadership Conference (SCLC) chose Selma, Alabama, as the site for renewed civil rights demonstrations. It was a superb choice. Selma was the county seat of Dallas County, Alabama. Although blacks com-

prised almost 58 percent of its population, only 2 percent of its
registered voters were black. Litigation under previous civil
rights legislation, including the 1964 Civil Rights Act, had
failed to alter the pattern of discrimination. Registration was
available to new voters only two days each month, and regis-
trants had to answer sixty-eight questions in order to qualify
to vote. Finally, Selma boasted a Neanderthal county sheriff in
the person of James Clark. Violently opposed to integration,
Clark radiated racial animosity and armed his deputies with
electric cattle prods. For King he was a godsend, because King
knew that violent suppression of nonviolent demonstrations
would rally apathetic moderates to his cause and compel the
president to act. As King's aide, Andrew Young, told Selma
marchers, "Actually, we're at war. We're trying to revolution-
ize the political structure in America."

Events proved him correct. It was war. On Sunday, March
7, 1965, a violent and bloody clash at the Edmund Pettus
Bridge, when Alabama state troopers and sheriff's deputies attacked peaceful civil rights demonstrators, shocked the nation
and roused President Johnson to action. A week later the president addressed a joint session of Congress to introduce voting
rights legislation. The 1965 Voting Rights Bill proposed to
eliminate the case-by-case approach against voting discrimination and to change dramatically the entire system once and
for all. Federal law would supplant state voter-registration
machinery wherever patterns of discrimination were evident.
Johnson argued that the "right to vote is the meat in the co-
conut. They can get the rest themselves if they get this—and
they can get it on their own terms, not as a gift from the white
man."

Even as he moved to support direct federal intervention in
the Deep South, however, Johnson did so under the umbrella
of consensus rhetoric. "The vote," he said, "is the most power-

ful instrument ever devised by man for breaking down injustice and destroying the terrible walls which imprison men because they are different from other men." Speaking in the same tone, Martin Luther King, Jr., argued: "Give us the ballot and we will transform the salient misdeeds of bloodthirsty mobs into the abiding good deeds of orderly citizens. Give us the ballot and we will fill our legislative halls with men of goodwill." Aaron Henry, longtime Mississippi civil rights activist, went even further: "My feeling is that all of the problems can be resolved once the right to vote is gained." Each of these men sought to soften the implications of revolutionary change by appealing to mainstream values. But there was more here than met the eye.

On its face the Voting Rights Bill was clear and direct. Because the 1964 Civil Rights Act already outlawed the use of literacy tests, the Voting Rights Bill sought to close other loopholes that Southern registrars had effectively used to deny voting rights. Section 2 prohibited basing the right to vote on race or color, essentially a restatement of the Fifteenth Amendment to the Constitution, adopted in 1870. The key was the punishment contained in Section 3, which outlined a "trigger formula" to invalidate tests or devices used to deny the right to vote. Any state or county that had less than 50 percent of its voting-age population either registered to vote or actually voting in the 1964 presidential election was obliged to suspend the use of restrictive registration procedures. As implemented by subsequent sections of the act, the attorney general could assign federal voting examiners to register voters in any area covered by the 50-percent formula. In addition, Section 5 of the bill prohibited any area covered by this trigger formula from changing any "electoral practices" without first "pre-clearing" those changes with the Justice Department or with the federal district court in the District of Columbia.

This provision not only took such decisions out of the hands of compliant Southern judges, it was automatic and did not require a political decision by any executive or legislative official. The drafters of the bill hoped this would prevent the dilution of blacks' electoral power after they had registered to vote. The states originally covered by this preclearance provision were Alabama, Georgia, Louisiana, Mississippi, South Carolina, Virginia, and parts of North Carolina.

Perhaps the most significant aspects of the bill were the preclearance section, which sought to rein in the white power structure, and the decision to eliminate the ongoing requirement of bringing individual lawsuits for particular areas and resort instead to blanket legislation. Voting examiners were not new; they had been a part of the 1960 Civil Rights Act. But the trigger mechanism was new, at once the most striking and the most controversial aspect of the legislation. As the historian Hugh Davis Graham noted, this hinted at a radical shift from "procedural to substantive criteria [the 50-percent formula] in civil rights law, from intent to effect, from equal opportunity to right to equality as a fact and as a result." The implications of such a shift were unclear.

The administration placed the Voting Rights Bill on a fast track through the Congress. The largest obstacle arose in the Senate, where James Eastland of Mississippi so dominated the Judiciary Committee that only one civil rights bill had come out of that committee in nine years. During the Senate debate Eastland warned that with passage of the bill the American people would witness the "domino theory right here at home," with one constitutional liberty after another falling "in rapid succession." The legislation would establish an "all powerful, unchecked, unanswered, supersocialist state." When that happened, Eastland warned, "the dark night of despotism will descend like a pall upon this great Nation and the rule of

tyranny will pervade the land." To prevent him from burying
the Voting Rights Bill, a majority of the Senate voted that the
bill be reported to the full Senate within fifteen days. As Attorney General Nicholas Katzenbach noted in testimony during the Judiciary Committee hearings in late March: "There
comes a time when the facts are all in, the alternatives have
been tried and found wanting, and time has run out. We stand
at that point today."

This did not deter the opposition. The *Wall Street Journal*
echoed the complaints of Southerners, calling the bill an "immoral law" that violated the Constitution. Senator Sam Ervin
of North Carolina spearheaded much of the Southern attack.
Ervin complained that the bill itself was discriminatory because it outlawed particular electoral practices *only* in states
with low voter turnout and small minority registrations. Indeed, unless the nonwhite voting-age population of any political subdivision surpassed 20 percent it was exempt from the
law; other states, therefore, could still employ literacy tests or
other discriminatory procedures. Judge Leander Perez of
Louisiana testified that the bill was "nefarious, willful, mali-
cious, lying propaganda." It was advocated by a "Communist
front" intent on carrying out "the original Stalin plan until the
time is ripe for revolution for self-determination in the Black
Belt." The right-wing Liberty Lobby went even further,
charging that if "the President's law is passed, the South will
disappear from the civilized world."

Republican Senator Jacob Javits of New York had an answer for the bill's critics. The United States faced a "burning
situation," he warned, and Congress could not simply stand
aside. It had to realize that "the times have caught up with us,
and great masses of the people will stand for it no longer." Determined to guarantee the right to vote, the Senate majority
overwhelmingly invoked cloture on May 25, even though the

Southern filibuster was still at best halfhearted. The next day the Senate approved the bill 77 to 19 and sent it to the House after only twenty-five days of debate. When the bill left the Senate it included several key amendments, among them a declaration that poll taxes abridged the right to vote as well as a provision that the right to vote could not be denied to individuals who had completed the sixth grade in an "American flag" school that was conducted in another language because of their inability to read or write English.

The House held its own hearings on the bill, allowing Southern Democrats to vent their outrage and opposition. W. J. Bryan Dorn of South Carolina railed against the preclearance procedures.

> This is the second time in approximately 1 year that the Congress and the country are being blackmailed and stampeded by threats of violence to pass ill-advised, ill-conceived, and unconstitutional legislation. This bill would make a mockery of the rights of the States, the local governments, the Constitution, and due process of law. This legislation would make a sham of our Democratic ideals in favor of mobocracy. This is punitive legislation. It is vindictive and sectional. It is evil legislation conceived in the minds of those who would vote masses of our people rather than permit them the choice of a free ballot.

"Compared to the long-term implications of the Voting Rights Act," complained Thomas G. Abernethy of Mississippi, "the civil rights act seems mild." Republican Jack Edwards of Alabama explicitly compared President Johnson's proposal to the efforts of Adolf Hitler during the 1930s in Germany.

Despite opponents' attacks, the bill sailed through the House with only a few amendments. On July 9, 1965, the House approved voting rights legislation 333 to 85 (76 of the 85 "no" votes came from Southerners) and sent the bill to conference committee. By early August both the Senate and House had adopted the conference report (328 to 74 and 79 to 18). The final bill retained the so-called American flag provision (which pertained chiefly to Puerto Rican voters in New York City) but agreed to drop the House-sponsored ban on poll taxes. The Senate had narrowly defeated a similar amendment, instead urging that the courts test the constitutionality of this issue and hopefully issue a nationwide ban. On August 6, 1965, President Johnson signed the Voting Rights Act.

Almost at once the legislation transformed the political landscape of the South. The administration quickly sent federal voting registrars into Alabama, Louisiana, and Mississippi; in three weeks they registered tens of thousands of new voters. Within three years black voter registration in Mississippi jumped from 6 to 44 percent. By 1976 it had risen almost nine times above 1964 levels. Much of this increase, however, stemmed from persistent registration efforts by various civil rights organizations, especially CORE (the Congress of Racial Equality), SNCC, and the NAACP. And the federal government never targeted some counties, largely for political reasons. Sunflower County, Mississippi, for instance, escaped entirely. Although it was the home county of MFDP activist Fannie Lou Hamer, it was also home to Senator James Eastland, powerful chairman of the Judiciary Committee. Indeed, within two years federal examiners had largely disappeared from the South. The Department of Justice blocked efforts by state courts in Alabama, Louisiana, and Mississippi to prevent the addition of newly registered voters to the rolls on the pretense that the activities of federal examiners violated those states' constitutions. In addition, the Justice Department immediately filed suit to eliminate poll taxes in Alabama, Mississippi, Texas, and Virginia.

In the wake of this new voter registration, several questions remained unanswered. Would the newly enfranchised black voters be able to translate their new voting strength into political power? Would historically black districts remain intact and elect black officials at the local and state levels, or would the white power structure find other ways to dilute the black vote and retain white officials in office? Was Lyndon Johnson right when he insisted that, once given the vote, blacks could now get anything else they needed? The power of the ballot held a hallowed place in American political mythology, but was this the coming of popular democracy to the South or only a persistent myth? Would civil rights leaders and, perhaps more important, the black population they had mobilized see enfranchisement as the fulfillment of their dreams, or as just another step along the way? In particular, would they consider it sufficient to address broader social and economic issues, such as employment opportunity, jobs, or housing discrimination? Finally, how would the Southern white population react? During the next three decades the answers to these questions gradually became evident.

One immediate response was that Southern whites flocked to registration centers. Due in no small part to people such as Governor George Wallace, in Alabama during the next three years more whites than blacks registered to vote. By 1967 more than 90 percent of age-eligible whites in Alabama were registered. Elsewhere, as in South Carolina, white Democrats rebelled against their party for its support of civil rights. The state had gone for Goldwater in 1964 and continued its shift into Republican ranks as its senior senator, Strom Thurmond, switched parties. Other areas of the South, however, displayed progress. In Houston, Texas, for example, Barbara Jordan finally won election to the state house from a majority-minority district after two unsuccessful efforts in at-large elections.

More important, by destroying white obstacles to black registration, the Voting Rights Act set in motion a long-term shift in the Southern political structure. Newly enfranchised black voters could now prevent a rollback of civil rights gains. Disfranchisement had played a major role in the erosion of progress after Reconstruction. The Voting Rights Act was designed to ensure that history would not repeat itself. The only alternative would have been a diminution of racial prejudice in the United States to the point that race was no longer a factor in voter preference. There was little evidence of this. In many respects, passage of this legislation began, not ended, the struggle to elect black officials, as whites responded to the new potential for black political power by exploring other ways to dilute black voting strength.

Passage of the 1964 Civil Rights Act and the 1965 Voting Rights Act cleared the way for passage of other Great Society legislation. President Johnson believed that since Congress had now attended to the burning issue of civil rights, it could turn to other important pieces of his Great Society. But five days after the president signed the Voting Rights Act, a riot erupted in the Watts section of Los Angeles. This racial outburst transformed the tenor of the civil rights issue for many white Americans, and in 1965 and 1966 popular concerns began to shift from civil rights to race. At the same time the civil rights movement moved northward, attacking *de facto* social and residential segregation in Northern cities and suburbs. As it did, defining the issue in moral terms became more difficult. Frustrated by slow progress, SNCC and CORE began to embrace black nationalism and exclude whites. Chants of "Black Power" echoed through crowds at demonstrations. Black Power advocate Stokely Carmichael warned that integration was "a subterfuge for the maintenance of white supremacy and reinforces, among both black and white, the idea that 'white' is automatically better and 'black' is by definiton inferior." This appealed particularly to younger blacks, such as the worker in Detroit who expressed his disenchantment with civil rights efforts: "I dig what Stokely Carmichael said. Whites appear to be friendly by passing a few laws, but my basic situation gets worse and worse. They don't really mean to change a thing." Charles Sherrod, an early civil rights activist, sounded a similar theme: "We are more prejudiced and bitter, frustrated and impatient and hateful than our parents because we have had more and seen more than our parents . . . and think we can get more than they did and we think we can get it now because we have done miracles."

In April 1965 Andrew Kopkind warned in the *New Republic* of a "danger in the growing gap between Negro expectations and achievements. . . . As frustrations grow, so will the demands for radical action." And as minority urban politicians gained power in the aftermath of the Voting Rights Act, they found they must address these frustrations and the influence of the Black Power movement in order to gain reelection, since their power base was in black rather than white communities. Whites felt rejected and threatened; a backlash grew.

To complicate matters, in his June 1965 commencement address at Howard University, President Johnson moved beyond the goals and promises of the earlier civil rights movement and endorsed equality of *result* as well as equality of opportunity. "You do not take a person who, for years, has been hobbled by chains and liberate him, bring him up to the starting line and then say, 'You are free to compete with all the others,' and still justly believe that you have been completely fair." At the core of his message lay his assertion that "it is not enough just to open the gates of opportunity. All our citizens must have the ability to walk through those gates. . . . We seek . . . not just equality as a right and a theory but equality as a fact and equality as a result."

This new initiative alienated some of LBJ's white supporters who opposed any hint of compensatory racial preference and began to call themselves "neoconservatives." Liberalism began to come apart at the seams, divided between removing racial discrimination and ensuring racial equality. But at the moment few among the public grasped the implications of Johnson's remarks. Only over the next decade did the outlines and implications of what came to be called affirmative action become evident.

Johnson's address drew on an administration report prepared by Daniel Patrick Moynihan that itself became the focus of controversy. Released later that summer, the Moynihan Report exploded into a storm of controversy with its argument that the weakening of the black family in slavery lay at the root of virtually all problems within the African-American community. Although concerned more with poverty than with civil rights, the report played an important role in shifting the debate from civil rights to race. In so doing it exposed further fissures within liberalism. On one side were those who argued that individual deficiencies were the root cause of prevalent social problems. Correct those deficiencies and you solve the problems. But this ran the risk of demonizing the deviants. On the other side were those liberals who insisted that the cause of the problems lay in the social structure itself, that American society embodied a structured inequality which persisted despite individuals' efforts.

In *The Negro Family: The Case for National Action*, Moynihan argued that the authority and stature of the black male had deteriorated to create a "pathological matriarchal situation which is beginning to feed on itself." Although this paralleled other studies of lower-class life begun in the 1930s, the

Moynihan Report appeared in a much more racially charged atmosphere. And Moynihan was blunt: "The deterioration of the Negro family is demonstrated by these facts: (a) nearly a quarter of urban Negro marriages are dissolved; (b) nearly one-quarter of Negro births are now illegitimate; (c) as a consequence, almost one-fourth of Negro families are headed by females, and (d) this breakdown of the Negro family has led to a startling increase in welfare dependency."

The implications of Moynihan's study for the civil rights movement were profound, if not always well understood. If what he said was true, even in part, then the elimination of legal discrimination could not produce racial equality. As NAACP general counsel Robert Carter noted, "Demonstrating in lunch counters did not give people money to buy a dinner." But Moynihan's critics, especially in the African-American community, focused more on his critique of dysfunctional family life than on his attack against discriminatory socioeconomic institutions. Opposition to the Moynihan Report effectively silenced further discussion of the problem for the remainder of Johnson's term and beyond. The president nonetheless articulated the core of Moynihan's message in his Howard University speech when he noted that "freedom is not enough. You do not wipe away the scars of centuries by saying: Now you are free to go where you want, do as you desire, and choose the leaders you please." But there is little evidence that the president fully understood the implications of his remarks.

Nothing sent shock waves through the white community, however, so much as the Watts uprising of August 1965. The problems were clear, if complex. In the words of one black nationalist: "The ghetto is no promised land. There are no jobs to be integrated into. There's no way to move to the so-called integrated areas. The accepted liberal means don't work. The white power structure has no intention of giving up anything without demands, and power yields only to power." Sharing power was quite different from sharing a drinking fountain, a lunch counter, or a bus station rest room. It was a concept that transcended any pretense of consensus, one that drew racial lines much more indelibly and unleashed a white belligerence that rejected nonviolent change.

The predominant image produced by Watts was that of angry, undisciplined blacks looting stores and starting fires. For many whites, the riots replaced the image of the courageous and persecuted freedom fighter with that of the dangerous, self-seeking rebel. Daniel Moynihan defined this shift sharply:

> It [Watts] threw the civil rights movement entirely off balance. Until then, theirs had been the aggrieved, the just, the righteous cause. In the South an old game had been going on with a new rule, imperfectly understood by whites, that the first side to resort to violence—lost. Now in the North the Negroes had resorted to violence, in a wild destructive explosion that shattered, probably forever, the image of non-violent suffering. And within hours of the signing of the Voting Rights Act. The same new rule applied. The civil rights movement could not explain Watts, and could not justify it.

Critics repeatedly cited the statistics: at least 34 dead, 1,000 injured, and more than 4,000 arrested. Property damage surpassed $200 million in a riot that involved approximately 35,000 adults. As Gerald Horne has noted in his study of the Watts riot, the government used more law enforcement and military personnel to stop the riot than it used to put down unrest in the Dominican Republic that same year.

President Johnson appointed former CIA director John

McCone to chair a commission to explore the reasons for the riot. Warren Christopher was appointed vice-chair to offset McCone's conservatism, but Johnson also created his own investigative team headed by Deputy Attorney General Ramsey Clark. The McCone Commission reached two key conclusions. First, like almost everyone else, it judged that outside groups or agitators did not cause the riot. It was a spontaneous outburst driven by a collection of "riff-raff" that represented only a fraction of the black population. Its second conclusion, that police had acted properly, was not as widely shared. The black community of Watts saw the police as an army of occupation. Policemen referred to sections of Watts as "charcoal alley" and called their billy clubs "nigger knockers." Whites, on the other hand, backed the police and emphasized the need for law and order. As pollster Samuel Lubell reported, since 1950 white voters had consistently supported racial peace over racial justice. The McCone Commission's two major conclusions implied that the underlying problem was one of law and order rather than a need for structural change to create jobs and improve housing. Two years later another group, the Kerner Commission, concluded that white racism rather than black lawlessness had sparked the riot.

More troubling for the future of race relations were the persistent images of the riot in the face of basic facts. Why, many asked, had Watts occurred on the heels of the two most far-reaching civil rights laws in American history? The answers were clear, if not pleasant. Watts typified a truism of race relations in the United States that the civil rights laws had yet to address—the multiple levels of the problem of civil rights. One was clearly defined as civil rights: equal access to public facilities and the right to vote. The 1964 Civil Rights Act and the 1965 Voting Rights Act had addressed this level of discrimination and set in motion the mechanisms to solve the problems. But neither bill touched another level, which involved what the white public understood more as racial preference than as civil rights. This entailed access to adequate housing, education, and jobs. All three were serious problems, not only in Watts but in other urban areas across the country.

Although the riot in Watts was the most notable of 1965, almost two dozen riots erupted in twenty cities throughout the country that year. They produced more than 10,000 arrests, more than 1,200 wounded, and 43 deaths. The next year casualties fell, but the number of incidents more than doubled. The mood of the country changed quickly. In 1965 combat troops had gone to the Watts section of Los Angeles. They had also gone to the Dominican Republic and to Vietnam. The years of peaceful change suddenly seemed to be ending. Decisions at home and abroad would be painful and demand sacrifice from the white majority. Even while black voter registration jumped by leaps and bounds across the South, opposition to administration initiatives in civil rights climbed steadily in the North. By 1966 the Gallup Poll revealed that more than half of all whites polled believed the Johnson administration was pushing integration too fast.

Events in 1966 further illustrated this shift from civil rights to race. In June James Meredith, who as a student had successfully integrated the University of Mississippi in 1962, marched through Mississippi to encourage black voter registration. The march evoked the moral crises that had prompted landmark legislation. But Meredith was gunned down shortly after setting out. Activist leaders of all stripes— Martin Luther King, Jr., of the SCLC (Southern Christian Leadership Conference), Floyd McKissick of CORE, and Stokely Carmichael of SNCC—quickly determined to complete Meredith's march from Memphis, Tennessee, to Jackson,

Mississippi. Chants of "Black Power" echoed along the march route. Militancy replaced the ideals of integration and accommodation.

In the summer of 1966 Martin Luther King, Jr., and the SCLC targeted Chicago to open their civil rights struggle in the North, announcing that Chicago "could become the metropolis where a meaningful nonviolent movement could arouse the conscience of this nation to deal realistically with the northern ghetto." King had some basis for optimism. Cook County, Illinois, where Chicago was located, had the largest black population of any county in the country. In addition, as the historian Roger Biles has pointed out, its public housing projects alone had more African-American residents than Selma, Alabama. But King's mid-July rally at Soldier Field in Chicago drew only about 30,000 people instead of the 100,000 he had anticipated. Chicago was not Birmingham. Its mayor, Richard Daley, as hard-nosed as his predominantly white ethnic police force, was as determined to maintain law and order as he was not to make concessions to King. He had effectively coopted much of the local black leadership by including them in his Democratic machine.

Chicago that summer was filled with riots and marches, marches and riots, as King pushed for housing reform and city authorities stonewalled him. King's efforts ended in early September when 250 people, protected by almost 3,000 National Guardsmen, marched through the white ethnic suburb of Cicero, Illinois, chanting Black Power slogans. Mobs showered them with debris and drove them back. King had met defeat. Nonviolent direct action had succumbed to violent white resistance. As Ralph James noted in his study of King's Chicago campaign, the "consequences of housing discrimination—black relegation to slums and higher rents for inferior shelter—were difficult to convey by marching with a police escort through a white neighborhood." No persuasive moral argument had shamed local authorities into an agreement.

President Johnson's effort to pass a 1966 Civil Rights Act met a similar fate. After the passage of historic legislation in 1964 and 1965, defeat of the 1966 bill by the same Congress reflected a stunning change in the national mood. Like King's march in Chicago, the bill focused on housing discrimination. Its key was Title IV, an open-housing provision that barred racial discrimination in the sale and rental of all housing. Other parts of the legislation barred discrimination in federal and state jury selection and empowered the attorney general to initiate suits to protect civil rights workers and advance desegregation. The House added an amendment to prohibit interstate travel to incite a riot, clearly a reflection of a shifting national consensus, before passing the bill by a margin of 259 to 157—a much smaller majority than had passed the Voting Rights Act.

The Senate refused to concur. Title IV was the linchpin, and it mightily offended Republican leader Everett Dirksen, who led opposition to the measure. Civil rights leaders had foreseen this possibility and had urged President Johnson to implement open housing through executive order rather than through legislation. LBJ, perhaps convinced that his majority was unshakable, insisted than an executive order might raise constitutional problems and that legislation was preferable. But when other Republicans joined Dirksen and a powerful real estate lobby to insist that a person's home was his castle, the bill was doomed. The Senate twice refused to vote cloture, and by September the bill was dead.

The 1966 congressional elections reflected rising white concern about the pace of racial change and the collapse of a civil rights consensus. As one presidential aide noted, "It would have been hard to pass the Emancipation Proclamation in the atmosphere prevailing this summer." The proliferation of Black Power doctrines alarmed whites, and when leaders such as Stokely Carmichael proclaimed that "When you talk about black power, you talk of building a movement that will smash everything Western civilization has created," whites became positively frightened. A white majority appeared to agree with President Johnson's earlier conclusion that blacks could get everything whites had now that the Civil Rights and Voting Rights Acts were law.

The midterm elections were a crushing defeat for congressional Democrats. Republicans gained forty-seven House seats and three Senate seats. The fact that over half the new Democrats elected in LBJ's 1964 landslide victory went down to defeat in 1966 was not in itself striking. Many came from marginal, even Republican, districts and owed their election more to Barry Goldwater than to Lyndon Johnson. But while Democrats still controlled the Congress (248 to 187 in the House; 64 to 36 in the Senate), the working liberal majority responsible for breaking the civil rights logjam and passing the liberal agenda was gone. Only 156 of the 248 House Democrats were Northerners who might consistently support the president. At the state level, racial conservatives scored significant victories. Lurleen Wallace succeeded her husband as governor of Alabama, and Ronald Reagan won election as governor of California. The elections pushed even Lyndon Johnson—a man determined to find the consensus position and locate himself there—to the right. A cleavage opened between liberal Democrats and Johnson's legislative initiatives. LBJ had adroitly used his lopsided majorities in the Eighty-ninth Congress to advance the Great Society, but he had failed to build the Democratic party so as to develop majorities in future Congresses.

The riots and election results had their most immediate impact on the Congress itself. Now more conservative, it more readily challenged the president's agenda and began to back away from earlier commitments almost before they had been implemented. For example, it restricted the ability of federal officials to withhold monies from school districts that had failed to integrate. A June 1966 White House conference on civil rights ended in failure. Although the 2,500 delegates called for an end to racial discrimination in housing, their final document (*To Fulfill These Rights*) failed to smooth over deep divisions in the civil rights movement or the growing opposition to the president's policies in Vietnam.

Meanwhile, implementation of the 1964 Civil Rights Act was moving to fruition. By April 1966 the EEOC had received five thousand complaints, though it had anticipated only two thousand during its first fiscal year. Its problem was clear: was it to apply specific remedies to specific cases, or was it to pursue an affirmative-action policy on a broader scale? The law itself seemed clear. Title VII proclaimed that preferential treatment and quotas were illegal. But the answer, as Hugh Davis Graham has noted, by 1966 was remarkably unclear. Was affirmative action, as Lyndon Johnson outlined it in his Howard University speech, possible without preferences or quotas?

In his 1967 State of the Union Message, and again in a special message on civil rights in mid-February 1967, President Johnson once more pushed his agenda that had failed the previous year. Fair housing remained the key provision of his civil rights bill, but this time LBJ proposed that the secretary of housing and urban development hold administrative hearings and issue cease-and-desist orders rather than pursue enforcement through the courts. Either way, Congress was not interested. In a midsummer article in the *New York Review of Books*, Andrew Kopkind reflected on what had happened:

"The maneuverings of the last half-decade have been predi-
cated on King's assumption that the American system can
somehow absorb the demands of its underclass and its alienated. Now this summer we all know that it cannot. Those
who speak in seats of power seem not to have the slightest idea
what those demands are, much less know how to meet them."

Early in 1968 the tide suddenly turned. The Senate took up
a fair-housing bill. By early March it had voted cloture to cut
off a Southern filibuster, then quickly passed the bill and sent
it on to the House, which accepted it intact so as to avoid a debilitating conference report. President Johnson signed the
measure on April 11, 1968. The act banned discrimination in
federally owned housing and in multi-unit buildings with
mortgages that were federally insured or underwritten.
Within a year discrimination in multi-unit dwellings was to
be illegal, though the act exempted owner-occupied buildings
with four or fewer apartments. By 1970 it would affect
all single-family homes rented or sold through real estate
brokers.

What had happened? Certainly one essential difference
was the support of Republican leader Everett Dirksen. A
wave of 128 urban riots in 1967, especially a devastating Detroit riot, had, in Dirksen's words, "put this whole matter in a
different frame." The report of the National Advisory Commission on Civil Disorders, chaired by Illinois Governor Otto
Kerner, defined the problem sharply: "Our nation is moving
toward two societies, one black, one white—separate and unequal." The public hungered for answers; more than 740,000
copies of the report were sold. The riots, according to the report, were political protests by angry ghetto blacks and not
revolutionary outbursts by undisciplined hoodlums.

Although the Senate seemed enlightened by the new wave
of urban rioting and passed the fair-housing bill by a margin

of 71 to 20, in the House the story was different. There the margin was much closer, and the measure passed in large part as an aftermath of Martin Luther King's assassination on April 4 and the accompanying violence across the country. Even then the bill passed by a margin of only 250 to 172, and contained tough language against urban rioters. It also failed to establish an enforcement mechanism for its provisions. Two months later the Supreme Court rendered these efforts somewhat unnecessary when it decided in *Jones v. Alfred H. Mayer Co.* that the Civil Rights Act of 1866 prohibited racial discrimination in housing.

Passage of the 1968 bill was a surprise, but it marked the end of Lyndon Johnson's civil rights enterprise. Clear evidence of the shift lay within the bill itself, which made interstate travel to aid or participate in a riot a federal crime. Title X of the bill also criminalized any demonstration of a firearm or explosive that might be used in a civil disorder. In short, the bill emphasized tough crime measures as much as it did fair housing. After passage, Congress denied all funding to implement its provisions. Not only had two years of urban riots fostered a strong white backlash against civil rights, but the movement itself was divided over personalities and philosophies. And the war in Vietnam had eroded Lyndon Johnson's presidency to the point of no return. In late March 1968 the president announced to the nation that he would not be a candidate in the fall elections.

Unlike other parts of his Great Society, civil rights did not run aground on the shoals of Vietnam. Its problems were many, but two stand out. First, white support for racial equality rested on a presumption of color-blind *opportunity* rather than *results*. Hence the Civil Rights Act of 1964 and the Voting Rights Act of 1965 received widespread biracial support because they promised to clear away obstacles and provide

African Americans with the opportunity to participate more fully in American society. Subsequent policies, which sought to move beyond this and equalize results, won much less support.

Second, the early stages of the civil rights movement rested on a clear dichotomy between the moral and the immoral. For most Americans in the early 1960s, that one had a right to use rest rooms, view movies, drink at a water fountain, ride buses, or eat in a restaurant without racial discrimination seemed clear. These were broad social arrangements that did not threaten one's own exercise of similar rights. But when the issues shifted to employment and housing, perceptions changed. Even in the halcyon economic climate of the mid-sixties, these "rights" appeared much more threatening on a personal level. An underlying conviction pervaded much of white America that such rights intruded in the private sphere and were unacceptable. So in 1968, when Lyndon Johnson issued an executive order requiring federal contractors to recruit and hire qualified minority job applicants, and when the Labor Department demanded that major contractors adopt a "written affirmative action compliance program," white opposition skyrocketed. Although the U.S. comptroller general rejected this "Philadelphia Plan," it would return in future years. Whites believed that affirmative action meant quotas, and quotas transcended equal opportunity. A battle was joined that still rages.

2

The War on Poverty

THE SECOND KEY to Lyndon Johnson's Great Society, and in many respects the nucleus, was the War on Poverty. Like the 1964 Civil Rights Act, it originated in the Kennedy administration, but by November 1963 an antipoverty commitment had yet to develop into a legislative program. The day after Kennedy's assassination, Johnson told Walter Heller of the Council of Economic Advisers to put poverty legislation on a fast track. "That's my kind of program," he told Heller. LBJ wanted to help people "who've never held real jobs and aren't equipped to handle them. . . . They were born to parents who gave up long ago. They have no motivation to reach for something better because the sum total of their lives is losing." In the words of Representative Charles Weltner of Georgia, "No one can walk through a slum, or smell the stench of poverty, or look into the eyes of the hopeless without sensing that duty" to help people in need. The president was not responding to a public groundswell but to his own vision of the Great Society and his paternalistic desire to improve the lives of all Americans. Johnson believed that the eradication of poverty would be his path to greatness as president.

Unlike civil rights, which rested on a moral consensus thrown into bold relief by the violent actions of Southern white officials against nonviolent blacks, the attack on poverty lacked a clear-cut consensus—aside, perhaps, from a belief that in the prosperous 1960s no one in the United States should be poor. Indeed, in a March 1964 Gallup Poll 83 percent of respondents believed that poverty would never disappear in the United States. But why were people poor in the first place? Was poverty the result of victimization, or was it self-inflicted? This was the crucial and ultimately divisive question. The public was split almost evenly between blaming the individual or blaming his circumstances and environment.

In his studies of the "underclass," Michael Katz has dissected the major issues central to the debate over poverty and the poor. They are perhaps best understood as a series of questions. To what extent are individuals responsible for their poverty? What is the role of culture in poverty? Indeed, is poverty behavioral and cultural, or is it structural, economic, and political? Do factors such as family structure and styles of child-rearing produce particular social pathologies? Do environmental factors drive "deviant" social values such as premarital pregnancy, school dropout rates, crime, or dependency? To what extent can institutions alter these factors? And, finally, can public policy actually eradicate poverty?

In the heady atmosphere of the early 1960s, social scientists believed they could devise policies to eliminate poverty in all but the most extreme cases by joining the analytical capacity of social science with the programmatic potential of public policy. After all, if President Kennedy's challenge to land a man on the moon by the end of the decade was realistic, surely social engineering could eradicate poverty at home. Several theories emerged to explain the persistence of poverty in the midst of prosperity, but even now there remains much disagreement over their validity. Many critiques of the antipoverty program focus as much on these theories as on the programs they spawned. Howard Phillips, a founding member of the conservative Young Americans for Freedom, whom Richard Nixon later hired to dismantle the Office of Economic Opportunity, best summarized the conservative attack: "The liberal conception of OEO was not primarily as an instrument for grappling with economic poverty, but rather as an institution which could finance the practice of liberal theories and support an extensive network of social welfare professionals and activists for socio-political change."

The most prevalent explanation for the poor was the culture-of-poverty theory. Advanced most strenuously in the writings of the anthropologist Oscar Lewis (*Five Families: Mexican Case Studies in the Culture of Poverty* [1959] and *The Children of Sanchez* [1961]), it argued not only that the poor were lazy and lacked ambition but that they passed on these traits to subsequent generations. The problem was therefore cultural rather than economic. This cultural explanation divorced the problem of poverty from economics. Michael Harrington, who called the poor the "other America," concluded that "the impoverished American tends to see life as fate, an endless cycle from which there is no deliverance." In short, lacking the necessary education or skills, the poor were trapped. Only by changing the environment of the young could the poor be given incentive to break this cycle. Give them opportunity, make them employable, and they would find their own jobs. Unleash the power of middle-class ideals and poverty would disappear.

A second theory of poverty focused on family structure. Here the landmark work belonged to Daniel Patrick Moynihan, who argued that children who grew up without a stable, two-parent family were likely to live a life of poverty. This "deviancy" bred a social pathology that, Moynihan insisted, was particularly virulent among African Americans. Not surprisingly, these ideas came under strong attack from the black community. James Farmer of CORE argued that Moynihan's well-intentioned analysis was fuel for "a new racism." It took the "tragedy of black poverty" and suggested that civil rights focus on "Negro mental health." Perhaps the problem, Farmer responded, was the "normal white family structure that is weaned on race hatred and passes the word 'nigger' from generation to generation."

Another idea that supported the War on Poverty focused on the linkage of race, class, and power. With the country in the midst of a civil rights revolution, as Elinor Graham has noted, emphasizing poverty shifted the focus from race to class. The question here, as the 1963 March on Washington demonstrated with its emphasis on jobs as well as racial equality, was whether the two might be joined. Indeed, the War on Poverty developed in part as a corollary to the civil rights movement. As that movement energized the black masses, an antipoverty program promised to provide jobs and forestall significant structural changes in the economy.

The coincidence of these two efforts led many whites to see antipoverty programs as an adjunct to the civil rights movement and poverty as a "black" issue, even though most of the poor were white. As particular elements of the president's War on Poverty became linked to struggles for political and economic power, this conviction strengthened. Many within the African-American community clearly understood that the two were fused. As one Harlem youth noted in 1960:

> So, all these frustrations build up within the black man day after day. The system that we live in becomes a vicious cycle and there is never a way out. He begs for change and it seems that the conditions get worse and worse and never make a move towards the better. And we find that for every step forward, we are forced by the powers that be to take five steps backward into even more deplorable condi-

tions. So, when this anger builds up in black people, not knowing how to let it out and how to retaliate against the power structures, the black man finds a way out; but the way out is often in the bottle of wine or in a needle containing heroin or in a reefer, or in the power of his fists when he slaps his wife down. The woman finds a way out in the power of her hand when she slaps a child down, and so the cycle goes on.

Greater participation in local politics, blacks believed, would empower them to take charge of their own destinies and create programs to help their communities directly. The danger here was that it frequently turned the debate away from the causes of poverty to the motivation for the poverty program itself. Was the program a response to black unrest and thereby a "reward" for riots? Or was the program (together with the 1965 Voting Rights Act) an effort to court the black vote and retain traditional Democratic strongholds in the face of white defections to the Republicans? Both explanations essentially argued that the antipoverty program was a crass, politically motivated effort to assure Democratic political hegemony. They also perpetrated a "social dissonance" theory of political change. That is, the only way to secure significant change was through confrontation and the threat or reality of violence. Class and racial divisions were so entrenched, this idea went, that those who "had" would not cede anything to those who "had not," except under extraordinary pressures.

There was, of course, another explanation—one that seemed to disappear as American society became increasingly polarized and violent in the late sixties. This was the possibility that the War on Poverty stemmed from compassion and goodwill, an attempt to rectify problems brought on by decades of discrimination and broad social forces at work in

American society. A black migration from South to North, rural to urban, had fundamentally altered the racial landscape of the United States after World War II. Geography, culture, race, the migration of industries from North to South, and the modernization of the American economy had combined to change the economic landscape. Even in the absence of public demands for corrective action, an antipoverty program emerged to ameliorate the hardships these changes had wrought—because it was the right thing to do.

As Michael Harrington pointed out in *The Other America* (1962), there was little doubt that a significant portion of the U.S. population lived in poverty. It included people who had lost their land, the elderly, minorities confronted by discrimination, workers displaced by industries that died or moved, children, and the poorly educated. Almost eleven million American adults had less than a sixth-grade education and could not read or write. In 1964 the Council of Economic Advisers found that one-fifth of all American families were poor, 78 percent of them white. One-third were headed by a person over age sixty-five, but almost half of all families headed by someone over sixty-five were poor. Although 54 percent of the poor lived in cities, more than 40 percent of all farm families were poor. Among nonwhites the percentage climbed to 80 percent. Almost half of female-headed families were poor, even though only a quarter of all poor families were headed by females. And they truly possessed little.

In 1962–1963 a family of four in Detroit on AFDC (Aid to Families with Dependent Children) was expected to survive on $160 per month. That amounted to $1,920 per year, well below the federal poverty level of $3,000 for a family of four. This meant that they lived on neck cuts for meat, did without fruits and vegetables, went without essential clothing such as raincoats or boots, had no telephones, and lacked money for health care. The chief cause of AFDC dependency, according to HEW statistics, was "the female-headed family with a live but absent father." In addition, illegitimacy rates tripled from 1940 to 1962, with the rate of increase for whites outpacing that for blacks in the 1950s. In January 1964 the Council of Economic Advisers reported that:

> The poor inhabit a world scarcely recognizable, and rarely recognized, by the majority of their fellow Americans. It is a world apart, whose inhabitants are isolated from the mainstream of American life and alienated from its values. It is a world where Americans are literally concerned with day-to-day survival—a roof over their heads, where the next meal is coming from. It is a world where a minor illness is a major tragedy, where pride and privacy must be sacrificed to get help, where honesty can become a luxury and ambition a myth. Worst of all—the poverty of the fathers is visited upon the children.

Welfare had become burdensome, however, and some conservatives rebelled against it. City Manager Joseph Mitchell of Newburgh, New York, advanced a plan to force able-bodied males back to work, deny benefits to unwed mothers who had another illegitimate child, and refuse benefits to individuals who came to his city without a firm offer of employment. Right-wingers in the Young Americans for Freedom and the John Birch Society hailed Mitchell's plan despite evidence that work could supplement but not replace welfare for most AFDC recipients. Although these ideas revived by the end of the 1980s, they were too extreme for the sixties. It was also largely political posturing. Only ten able-bodied males were on relief in Newburgh, and somewhere between 2 and 9 percent of the city's population collected welfare. For most Americans the promise of prosperity still loomed large; what was missing was a plan to distribute its benefits more equitably.

As Lyndon Johnson developed his antipoverty legislation in 1964, he faced several possible choices. He could conclude that the problem lay with individuals who possessed insufficient skills to get good-paying jobs. In that case the corrective would be to support job-training programs and educational opportunities. So long as the economy continued to expand (and this was the rationale for the 1964 tax cut), these programs would not affect the nonpoor at all. Since they completely avoided the question of income redistribution, they would also assure middle-class liberals and conservatives that nothing was fundamentally wrong with the country's economic system, the system they credited for their own prosperity. This focus on individual rehabilitation, especially the neglect of the working poor, would isolate the poverty population from the working class and thereby fracture the natural community of interest between the two. It also fit well with the culture-of-poverty theory to which Lyndon Johnson subscribed.

Another policy choice was to embrace a set of income transfer programs. While conservatives denounced this as "socialistic," even for liberals it risked contradicting their belief in the value of individual effort. More troubling, it directly blamed neither the system nor the individual, but "circumstances." If individuals lacked education or training, it would provide neither, and if something was structurally wrong with the system, it would not change that system. It was probably the worst of both worlds in the sense that it ameliorated the impact of poverty but failed to affect its causes.

Finally the president could embrace a program to change the nation's economic and political structure so that all Americans shared more equally in its rewards. In the midst of prosperity, and after almost two decades of expanding suburbia and a broadening middle class, the administration did not see this as a viable political alternative.

On March 16, 1964, Lyndon Johnson sent Congress a special message declaring war on poverty, emphasizing the need for all citizens to share in the opportunity of America. "We have come a long way toward this goal," he said. "We still have a long way to go. The distance which remains is the measure of the great unfinished work of our society." The War on Poverty would complete that work. The president submitted the Economic Opportunity Bill of 1964 to Congress because "it is right, because it is wise, and because, for the first time in our history, it is possible to conquer poverty." Winning was possible, Walter Heller argued in his subsequent testimony before the House Subcommittee on the War on Poverty Program, because the United States possessed the three ingredients essential to victory: material resources, human resources, and economic techniques. "All that is required," he concluded, "is the will to do the job and the specific ways to strike at the stubborn roots of poverty."

The president proposed a multifaceted bill whose first provision was the creation of a Job Corps. Essentially a work-training program, it built on the Manpower Development and Training Act passed during the Kennedy administration and was modeled in many respects on the Civilian Conservation Corps of New Deal years. Young men (women were excluded at the outset) would go to rural and urban residential centers to learn new skills. This removed them from family and neighborhood and reflected a suspicion that environmental factors fed the cycle of poverty. Title I, which included the Job Corps, created work-training programs for unemployed youth as well as work-study programs for students in colleges and universities.

The legislation also included—

Title II: Community Action Programs, adult basic education programs, and voluntary assistance programs for needy children ("to strike poverty at its source");

Title III: Programs to fight rural poverty and provide assistance for migrants and their families;

Title IV: Employment and investment incentives for small business;

Title V: Work Experience Programs for unemployed fathers and mothers to break "the pattern of poverty";

Title VI: Volunteers in Service to America (VISTA), a domestic peace corps to fight poverty at home.

The bulk of the money to be spent under the act ($727 million of the $962 million requested the first year) was earmarked for programs under Titles I and II, and most of that could already be found elsewhere in the administration's budget.

All of this would be run from a new Office of Economic Opportunity, created in the Office of the President. This centralized decision-making in the White House and essentially removed Congress from the policymaking loop. In closing his message to Congress, Johnson argued that the program was "within our means" but admitted that it would not "eliminate all the poverty in America in a few months or a few years. Poverty is deeply rooted and its causes are many." Nonetheless, privately LBJ worried about the problems of coordinating such a program which cut across the responsibilities of several cabinet officials, and he was unsure he could get even a $500 million appropriation through Congress.

The administration proceeded to blitz Congress with high-powered testimony about the far-ranging effects of poverty. The parade of witnesses was as impressive as their testimony was haunting. Secretary of Defense Robert McNamara cited Selective Service studies that one of every three young men failed to meet minimum physical and mental standards, and that this failure was often directly related to poverty. The men lacked education and had never received adequate medical attention. Secretary of Labor Willard Wirtz testified that 730,000 youths between the ages of sixteen and twenty-one were out of school and unemployed. Another 350,000 (what he called the "lost battalion") were out of school and completely outside the work force. Job growth had not kept pace with the rising population of young people, and in 1964 the leading edge of the baby boom was just turning eighteen.

Robert Kennedy, still attorney general, noted that by 1960, 59 percent of the West Virginia children who had started first grade twelve years earlier had dropped out of school. Poverty undercut education, and Kennedy argued that it contributed to juvenile delinquency, alcoholism, drug addiction, illiteracy, poor housing, and crime as well as unemployment. Poverty led to a sense of powerlessness, which was the handmaiden of despair. Walter Reuther, president of the United Auto Workers, went further and argued for national economic planning to achieve labor's long-sought goal of full employment. Mayors of key cities—Richard Daley of Chicago, Jerome Cavanagh of Detroit, Robert Wagner of New York—threw their support behind the measure, seeing it as a way not only to secure greater federal funds for their communities but to control the rising costs of welfare.

Critics of the proposed legislation, chiefly Republicans, bought none of this. Wisconsin Republican Melvin Laird charged that the bill was only "a transparent attempt to give a new look to the warmed-over policies of the 1930s." Peter

Frelinghuysen of New Jersey warned that the antipoverty program was a "patchwork of the worst kind." Ohio's Robert Taft, Jr., speaking to his colleagues, was more blunt:

> I guess that you realize by now that you are in the middle of what is a political hassle. I think you should recognize it is a political hassle in an election year. The hassle arises, and certainly I share some feeling of frustration in this bill, because the bill generally represents a new package, a new ribbon, and a new tag put around specific proposals that have been presented to the Congress previously and have failed to pass on their own merits.

Taft's colleagues warned that should the War on Poverty be launched, it would be long and expensive.

But, as the National Association of Manufacturers argued in its critique, this produced a dilemma. If "the program were to be expanded so as to reach all the cases it is intended to help," the NAM noted, "it would have to be many times larger. The cost would then reach a point where it would seriously impede the growth of the private economy. Thus you seem to have a choice between a program which is so small as to be ineffective, and one so large as to be damaging." The NAM, of course, opposed the whole idea of a war on poverty. Its solution to the poverty problem was simple and old-fashioned: reduce taxes, cut government spending, maintain the value of the dollar, reduce the power of labor, and have the states and localities provide public assistance where absolutely necessary. This relied on the old formula of economic growth as the cure for all economic and social ills, even though poverty had persisted despite years of postwar growth. Representative Frelinghuysen warned that the bill would "inevitably create great expectations but without the substance to satisfy such hopes."

The focus for much of the debate was the Community Action Program (CAP), which was to mobilize community resources to fight poverty. The idea for the Community Action Agencies (CAAs) stemmed from the work of David Hackett, who headed the President's Committee on Juvenile Delinquency and Youth Crime, and Richard Boone, who had been involved with the Ford Foundation's "Gray Areas" program. Both men believed that "local governments were themselves unresponsive to the poor," and that local initiatives were useful in stimulating independence and instituting change. But they also recommended starting with perhaps 10 or 20 pilot programs rather than a full-blown national effort in 250 cities. Behind their recommendations was the question of whether political empowerment was the path to economic security.

The community action debate centered on two aspects of the proposal. First was the purpose of the Community Action Agencies. They were to provide for the "maximum feasible participation of the poor" in developing and directing programs to relieve poverty. Their intent, in short, was to produce social change through participatory democracy. As such, they promised to empower individuals at the grass roots who had long been denied power—thereby threatening existing political power structures and social welfare agencies. Second, to the extent that Community Action Agencies received power and money, they had resources attractive to community activists who now sought places on CAA boards. They did so at the very moment that the nature of reform movements in the country, especially the civil rights movement, was changing. As civil rights groups moved toward Black Power, and as Community Action Agencies became a potential base for political power, both converged to threaten local power structures. If community action was conceived as a means to contain racial militancy, it proved to have just the opposite effect. Big-city mayors came to regret their support for this section of the bill.

One important example of how community action represented both the promise and the problem of antipoverty efforts was the experience of Newark, New Jersey. During the summer of 1964 the New Left, under the auspices of SDS (Students for a Democratic Society), had launched the Newark Community Union Project (NCUP) as one of ten Economic Research and Action Projects (ERAPs). This was partially a reaction to SNCC's move to exclude whites from its Southern organizing efforts. The NCUP used white SDS organizers to mobilize the poor in Northern cities. Under the early direction of Carl Wittman and Tom Hayden, the NCUP was one of the most important ERAP projects. Wittman and Hayden quickly discovered, however, that most of the area residents were African-American and Puerto Rican rather than white, and that the majority were working class and middle class rather than poor and unemployed. But neither of these facts undermined ERAP efforts; the real problem for SDS proved to be the implacable hostility of the business and political establishment of Newark, including the liberal community. Hayden and Wittman complained in their report on the project that "Our initial experience has been with extremely self-serving people who have wide community contact but no active and radical membership base. Their aspirations are for political self-aggrandizement and orthodox liberal reforms. . . . In general, their program would do very little to change the real lives of the poor." Not everyone shared a desire for structural change.

The Economic Opportunity Bill easily cleared the Senate Labor and Public Welfare Committee, with only conservative Republicans Barry Goldwater (Arizona) and John Tower

(Texas) voting against it. The bill was never in doubt and passed Congress largely intact by late August. Voting in both the House (226 to 185) and the Senate (61 to 34), however, demonstrated stubborn Republican opposition.

The new act authorized ten specific programs, some of which were extensions of existing ones. Federal agencies other than the Office of Economic Opportunity (OEO) were to direct six of them: the Neighborhood Youth Corps (Labor Department), the Work Experience Project (Department of Health, Education and Welfare, HEW), the Adult Basic Education Program (HEW), the Rural Loan Program (Agriculture Department), the Small Business Loan Program (Small Business Administration), and the College Work Study Program (HEW). OEO itself would operate the remaining programs: the Job Corps, VISTA, the Community Action Program, and the Migrant Assistance Program.

To avoid last-minute public controversy, President Johnson delayed making grants under the legislation until he had coasted to victory in the November elections. But he need not have worried, because the white backlash against civil rights in the South failed to spread to economic matters, except insofar as the War on Poverty later became identified in the public mind as a program essentially for African Americans. Economic data clearly indicate that white blue-collar workers suffered no economic disadvantage from the extension of opportunity to their black counterparts. Between 1965 and 1969 the real median earnings of married, white, blue-collar workers rose by 15 percent. This rate was higher than that for any other category of married white males.

The Economic Opportunity Act sought to give Americans a chance to escape poverty and prepare young people for education and work. Those seemed to be noncontroversial goals, and in theory they were. But practice was something else again. The act suffered from hasty preparation, an absorption with racial and urban problems, and a failure to confront the underlying causes of poverty. Consequently its proposals were fragmented. Each section of the act sought a separate remedy to the problem of poverty, thus no coordinated program emerged. Given the lack of agreement about the roots of poverty, perhaps this was inevitable. Less inevitable, but understandable in the context of the times, was the act's focus on the black urban poor. This was not its original intent but quickly became its practice. Convinced that economic growth would be sufficient to create opportunities, the antipoverty program targeted *preparation* for jobs rather than the *creation* of jobs. As the target population came to be defined more by race than by income, white support for the endeavor declined.

The decision-making behind the creation of OEO, perhaps inadvertently, contained the seeds of future confrontation. As Adam Yarmolinsky, one of the architects of the War on Poverty, noted, "Our tactical decision was, let's concentrate first on preparing people for jobs." In rejecting the alternative backed by Labor Secretary Willard Wirtz, creating jobs for people, antipoverty planners decided not to confront directly the obstacles obstructing opportunity. When the approach later changed, a commitment to affirmative action drove a racial wedge into the working class. And because Title VI of the 1964 Civil Rights Act prohibited racial discrimination in employment, the federal government had a potent legal weapon to enforce its guidelines.

Congress appropriated only $800 million to fight the War on Poverty in its first year, and this at the very end of the session. Although the raw numbers of participants appeared large at first glance, the war was, as most observers have noted, really only a skirmish. Of the millions of Americans trapped in poverty, the War on Poverty touched fewer than 1 percent of them in its first year. The response overwhelmed the ability of the program to accommodate applicants. In the long run, experts noted, a more effective war on poverty might cost as much as $30 billion a year. Even LBJ's vision of a Great Society was not that grandiose, though he intended antipoverty expenditures to grow annually. In his mind that growth would not impinge on other programs because a steady annual expansion of the economy would make available additional federal revenues. Indeed, only by prescribing such a pain-free road to opportunity—a no-loss assumption by the middle class—could he maintain his consensus. When that assumption ceased to be viable, support for the War on Poverty waned.

The Appalachia Aid Bill of 1965 was the first Great Society legislation enacted by the Eighty-ninth Congress. It focused on regional development for the depressed twelve-state Appalachian region, covering all of West Virginia and parts of Alabama, Georgia, Kentucky, Maryland, North Carolina, Ohio, Pennsylvania, South Carolina, Tennessee, and Virginia. An Appalachian Regional Commission coordinated projects to develop the infrastructure by building roads, health facilities, and restoring natural resources. More than any other part of the War on Poverty, this bill reflected what most Americans thought the problem of poverty represented and what John Kennedy had articulated following the 1960 primary campaign in West Virginia. This "other American" was predominantly white and rural. That image soon changed. By 1968 blacks dominated the ranks of most OEO employment programs, representing 47 percent of the Neighborhood Youth Corps, 59 percent of the Job Corps, and 81 percent of the Concentrated Employment Programs.

Within a year after the War on Poverty began, several problems emerged to undermine its efforts. One was the mat-

ter of urban politics. Philadelphia had proposed an antipoverty program that channeled funds through traditional
political and social agencies, but OEO sent the city's mayor
back to the drawing board. The plans of other cities—New
York, Cleveland, Los Angeles, San Francisco—also met rejec-
tion. In January 1965 the U.S. Conference of Mayors asked the
president to curb the community action bureaucrats and to
vest control of local antipoverty programs with existing local
political authorities. Syracuse Mayor William Walsh (a Republican), faced by aggressive community organizers trained
by radical activist Saul Alinsky, warned that "We are experiencing a class struggle in the traditional Karl Marx style in
Syracuse, and I do not like it." Alinsky also attacked Chicago
Mayor Richard Daley's political use of War on Poverty funds,
citing it as evidence that the entire venture was nothing more
than a "prize piece of political pornography." Alinsky was
largely correct; the poor controlled only 1 or 2 percent of the
CAPs. More to the point, at least for the president, was that
these urban mayors constituted the backbone of the Democratic party, and they were exceedingly angry.

What was community action supposed to be? In their study
of OEO, Gordon Davis and Amanda Hawes outlined four
separate concepts of the program. One was the "Bureau of the
Budget" concept, which emphasized efficiency and coordination. Another they called the "Alinsky Concept," which
would disrupt the status quo to empower the poor. Third was
the "Peace Corps" concept, a vision that rested on services to
eliminate poverty much as had been done abroad. Finally
there was the "Task Force" concept, which essentially meant a
program that would pass Congress and be politically effective.
At one time or another all four of these concepts seemed to operate simultaneously in OEO, but since they were often mutually exclusive they led to confusion.

A lack of planning, combined with the scope of the programs, also proved troublesome. Thanks to Democratic Congresswoman Edith Green of Oregon, the requirement that cities submit comprehensive plans before receiving funds had not survived congressional scrutiny of the original legislation. In addition, War on Poverty chief Sargent Shriver and President Johnson rejected suggestions for pilot programs in a limited number of areas. They wanted a full-scale war, not a series of probing attacks. Now, as Shriver called for a long-range plan to create jobs, economic studies of job-creation programs revealed their high costs. At the same time Lyndon Johnson had begun sending U.S. ground troops to Vietnam. Although he managed to hide the true costs of this other war from the Congress for a while, LBJ knew what they might be and remained cautious about his future antipoverty budget requests.

Support for the Job Corps wavered as the success rates of its participants failed to meet expectations and the dropout rate rose. There were clear explanations for these problems, but each one only demonstrated how difficult was the eradication of poverty. The Job Corps trained most of its recruits for service jobs, and neither wages nor job opportunities were particularly good in that sector of the economy. In addition, the Job Corps worked with the hard-core unemployed. Its recruits suffered not only from a history of impoverishment but lacked education and the mental skills that might make them readily employable. Nearly a third of the enrollees could not read a simple sentence; 60 percent came from broken homes; 40 percent were from families on relief; half could not complete reading or arithmetic above a fifth-grade level.

Establishment of the Legal Services Program under OEO also created controversy. This initiative was designed to provide the poor with the same legal opportunities enjoyed by

wealthier citizens. Although Legal Services was part of the
Community Action Program, this connection was not its only
source of difficulty. What Legal Services did, or threatened to
do, was empower the poor to fight the "system" on its own
terms. Despite its failure to democratize access to the legal system, it provided the poor with a weapon to overcome their
sense of helplessness. Edgar and Jean Cahn, who helped plan
the program, argued in an important 1964 *Yale Law Journal*
article that the "ultimate test . . . is whether or not the citi-
zenry have been given the effective power to criticize, to dissent, and, where need be, to compel responsiveness." In short,
Legal Services challenged existing economic, political, and social structures.

By 1966 the ideals of 1964 had faded. Although the number
of people in poverty fell between 1965 and 1970, from about 33
million to 25 million, critics attacked the War on Poverty.
Lloyd Ohlin, an architect of the program, had observed in
1964 that the "good society" was "one in which access to opportunities and the organization of facilities and resources are
so designed as to maximize each individual's chance to grow
and achieve his greatest potential for constructive contribution
to the cultural life of the social order." Two years later the soci-
ologist Nathan Glazer concluded that there were "limits to
the desirable reach of social engineering." New York's liberal
Republican Mayor John Lindsay outlined the implications of
this shift:

> . . . This decade began with an essentially secure sense that
> there was a vital, responsive center, alert to grievances,
> open to dissent and suasion. And as it ends, there is around
> us a sense of disaffection and betrayal. More and more of
> those who labored in mainstream politics only two years
> ago argue now that those in authority simply will not per-
> mit a real challenge to their power. . . . Now this current of

doubt has spread beyond the campus and the ghetto. It flows in the broad mainstream of American life as well. It is as though this nation, strong and blessed, had suddenly been stripped of its protection, exposing our people to doubt and threat. . . .

Thus the final problem: disenchantment. Perhaps Americans always wanted a quick fix; perhaps the president had oversold the antipoverty program; perhaps the appearance of a more strident militancy among civil rights groups, youthful activists, and antiwar protestors led middle-class voters to value social peace over social change.

Still, parts of the War on Poverty attracted support. The Head Start Program in particular found widespread public acceptance and reached more than half a million children in 1965, its first year of operation. It aimed to put poor preschool children on an equal footing with their nonpoor peers when they entered primary school, through preschool classes. But there was more to this than education. In the words of one observer, "Head Start teachers transmitted basic learning experiences to children who in many cases had never opened a book or touched a pencil, had never eaten an apple or used a knife and fork, and, in some cases, had never talked because no one had talked to them. Many did not recognize colors and could not identify everyday objects." Medical examinations for children in the Jacksonville, Florida, Head Start program revealed the pernicious impact of poverty: 52 percent were anemic, 45 percent lacked dental care, 31 percent had hearing defects, 25 percent suffered from eye troubles, and 5 percent were partially blind. Testimony by Dr. Donald Gatch at an antipoverty hearing in November 1967 revealed that underfed African-American children in South Carolina were dying of parasitic diseases. In that state's Beaufort County a study

found that 90 percent of the children under age five suffered
from hookworms and roundworms. Another study in Boston
discovered that 31 percent of Head Start children suffered
major physical or emotional problems.

In the South, Head Start promised to elevate the educational level of minority students, and it found an unquench-
able educational thirst. In his study of poverty law, Sar
Levitan noted that while there were "twice as many poor
white families in the South as poor nonwhite families, Negro
children have constituted the majority of Head Start participants in the South." The program was popular because it extended educational opportunity to groups long denied it, and
because early studies clearly indicated that it worked. A study
of participants in Baltimore's 1965 Head Start project revealed
that the children gained eight to ten points on their IQs. Although by the end of the decade social scientists questioned its
lasting value, noting that early advantages faded within three
to four years, early-childhood intervention remained the most
popular OEO program. Upward Bound programs and Pre-
College Enrichment programs used summer schools to prepare underprivileged students for college work by enhancing
their basic skills.

Amid the fast-paced change of the mid-sixties, the very existence of Head Start often contained the seeds of controversy.
Nowhere was this more evident than in Mississippi. The Ku
Klux Klan burned crosses at Head Start centers and at the
homes of Head Start teachers. Senator John Stennis led an effort to eject Head Start from the state when he launched an attack on the Child Development Group of Mississippi
(CDGM). The CDGM had received an OEO grant to provide
educational opportunities, but Stennis argued that it would
"play into the hands of extremists" and that OEO money was
underwriting "the extreme leftist civil rights and beatnik

groups in our state, some of which have definite connections with Communist organizations." Together with his colleague, Senator James Eastland, Stennis demanded the abolition of CDGM. What he really objected to was its support for civil rights. OEO, on the other hand, considered the CDGM a model because it delivered medical care, education, and nutritional nourishment to thousands of underprivileged children.

The CDGM did have its problems, and in 1966 controversy flared between CDGM and OEO. The central issues, apart from complaints from Stennis, Eastland, and other Mississippi political officials, was that CDGM was not sufficiently integrated (it needed more white children and white teachers), had alleged financial irregularities, and used federal vehicles for purposes other than Head Start. Absent was any complaint that its program was insufficient or inadequate. A biracial group of "loyal" Democrats, headed by Governor Paul Johnson and named Mississippi Action for Progress (MAP), applied to OEO for funding to replace CDGM. Its attitude was reflected in Governor Johnson's comment that "Nobody is starving in Mississippi. The nigra women I see are so fat they shine." In October 1966 Sargent Shriver announced that OEO would fund MAP rather than CDGM, despite protests from CDGM supporters. By December, with mediation from Vice-President Hubert Humphrey, OEO agreed to refund CDGM. After a five-month battle, CDGM endured. But in some ways the conflict in Mississippi resembled the one over the MFDP at Atlantic City in 1964. LBJ seemed more interested in placating the powerful and the entrenched than in fostering change. The near success of the MAP challengers further alienated some people from the "system" and lent credence to more radical alternatives.

The Economic Opportunity Amendments of 1965 reflected the continuing support of Congress despite critics' attacks.

They passed the House by twice the margin of the original bill the preceding year. Partisan divisions marked the voting. Republicans particularly attacked the Community Action Program, complaining that it had become a political pork barrel serving urban political bosses and their machines. The GOP, led by Representatives Charles Goodell (New York) and Albert Quie (Minnesota), launched an "Opportunity Crusade." They sponsored legislation to create a three-member Council of Economic Opportunity Advisers to the President, establish military centers to train volunteers to meet Selective Service standards, encourage states to contribute funds to Community Action Programs, legislate tax incentives for industry to train the unskilled, and replace the Job Corps with an "Industry Youth Corps" using employer tax credits to create new jobs for unemployed youth. The effort failed in Congress.

After riots in several Job Corps camps and numerous instances of "bureaucratic bungling," Congress granted governors the power to veto Job Corps and volunteer projects in their states. This was a slap at the Community Action Programs as well as at the growth of federal power. During the next three years governors in ten states vetoed thirty OEO grants. George and Lurleen Wallace of Alabama and Ronald Reagan of California accounted for 60 percent of these vetoes. Despite such setbacks, Congress nearly doubled its authorization of funds for 1965, agreeing to spend $1.5 billion for OEO programs.

The administration deliberately sought to avoid controversy in other OEO efforts. Particularly sensitive was the issue of family planning. By 1965 OEO had indicated a willingness to include funds for local birth-control projects as part of its War on Poverty, but it carefully limited their use to voluntary participants. Even though a National Academy of Sciences survey had shown that 95 percent of American couples favored family planning, and that even 80 percent of Catholic couples used it, OEO restricted family planning projects to married women and provided information only on the various types of birth control. When Catholic officials in Milwaukee opposed efforts to start a local birth-control clinic, the agency rejected the clinic's application.

An unforseen by-product of the War on Poverty was the discovery of even more poor people. "We have a rift between the haves and have-nots in this country that I have not seen in all my lifetime," warned Mary E. Switzer of the Department of Health, Education and Welfare. This was "an extremely ominous situation." Even though the government had launched an antipoverty program, poverty had not been a topic for serious study in the postwar United States. The more people looked at poverty, the more they found and the more complex it became.

A special committee of the Fund for the Republic warned that the United States was experiencing a "Triple Revolution" of cybernation, weaponry, and human rights. This meant, they concluded, that "the traditional link between jobs and income is being broken." What were the implications? At the very least, fundamental changes were reconfiguring economic and social patterns. The stopgap measures envisioned by the War on Poverty were woefully inadequate. As people realized that the future would not be like the past, they were likely to retract their commitments and convert their social idealism to self-protection, thus widening existing disparities. Some economists, including conservatives such as Milton Friedman of the University of Chicago, proposed instituting a "negative income tax" to guarantee individuals a certain level of income "as a matter of right."

In 1966 and after, Congress's enthusiasm for the War on Poverty cooled. House Democrats had to rally their forces to overturn a vote killing antipoverty funds for 1967. Even when Congress agreed to continue the program that year, it inserted new restrictive language, such as a prohibition on the provision of any funds or services "to anyone convicted of inciting or participating in a riot or of engaging in activity resulting in damage to property or persons." Increasingly mired in Vietnam, President Johnson seemed content to have launched the War on Poverty but refused to fight it through to the finish and did not push hard for his programs.

Sargent Shriver remained optimistic that OEO would end poverty in the United States by 1976, but few agreed with him. Longtime black activist A. Philip Randolph, president of the Brotherhood of Sleeping Car Porters, proposed a ten-year "freedom budget" of $185 billion to accomplish Shriver's goal. Numerous civil rights organizations—the NAACP, SNCC, CORE, SCLC, the Urban League—backed Randolph's proposal, but elsewhere it fell on deaf ears. For fiscal 1966 the administration cut OEO funding requests by nearly 50 percent even before submitting them to Congress. OEO was besieged on all sides. Black militants demanded more money and more control; the white establishment demanded controls exercised through traditional political channels at state and local levels. Conservatives, and some liberals, now understood the implications of "maximum feasible participation" and recoiled from them. They adopted an amendment sponsored by Democrat Edith Green, limiting representation of the poor on CAP boards by distributing one-third of the seats to public officials and other seats to private-sector representatives. With OEO in political difficulty by 1967, Congress extended the act for two more years only after a bitter struggle. Surprisingly, the House vote of 247 to 149 for extension included support from 40 percent of the Republicans.

Despite this reauthorization, a fear of being "for" poverty

did not still critics' voices. Some complaints were primarily partisan, but several developments fueled a rising tide of criticism against the War on Poverty and OEO in particular. One was a Bureau of the Budget decision in October 1965 requiring every federal agency to create an office for a Planning, Programming, Budgeting System. Its purpose, modeled after the system installed by Defense Secretary Robert McNamara at the Pentagon, was to assess statistically the effectiveness and efficiency of every government program. Here was social science raised to an art form. Never before had such an evaluation system been instituted, and it virtually guaranteed controversy. Not only were statistical measures of human progress likely to be misleading, they inevitably contained "evidence" to sustain numerous (often conflicting) interpretations. They also reinforced the tendency to look for quick results, avoid experimental programs that might fail, and then interpret any failure as evidence that the problem was intractable.

The release of studies on the impact of compensatory education also fueled criticism of OEO, particularly of Head Start. The most significant was the 1966 report on *Equality of Educational Opportunity*, known as the Coleman Report because James Coleman of Johns Hopkins University had directed the study. All the reports sounded a similar theme: that pupil achievement was more directly related to the students' home life than to the quality of their education. Opponents of OEO not only embraced these conclusions but took them to the extreme and argued that all antipoverty programs—indeed OEO itself—should be scrapped. Although later studies by the Cornell Consortium presented contradictory evidence that early childhood programs *did* have lasting effects, the Coleman Report became a potent weapon in the hands of critics of the OEO.

Critics of OEO also benefited from popular reaction to the rash of urban riots that dotted the country, especially in 1967 when 164 race riots erupted in the first nine months. Sargent Shriver and other OEO supporters blamed Vietnam war spending for some of OEO's problems. They noted that between 1965 and 1972 more than $128 billion was spent on Vietnam, compared to only $15 billion for the War on Poverty. But Shriver's lament that "Vietnam took it all away, every goddamned dollar; that's what killed the war on poverty" was misleading.

The riots produced a marked shift in public opinion. Many now thought that poverty spending "rewarded" blacks for rioting and should be eliminated in favor of law-and-order measures. LBJ's dilemma was apparent when he announced a new job-creation program after the 1967 riots. Called JOBS (Job Opportunities in the Business Sector), it sought to train the poor for jobs in the private sector. Eighteen months after its inception it had successfully placed 150,000 of the poverty-stricken unemployed in jobs, but it had also become essentially a program for blacks. This lent credence to critics' charges that JOBS was a civil rights–related program that rewarded rioters for their illegal behavior.

How are we to assess the War on Poverty? Was it only a skirmish? Were its programs essentially a series of "case studies" that sought to explore various theoretical avenues by which one might eliminate poverty? Inevitably there are more questions than answers, because measurements are imprecise. But several conclusions seem reasonable. Whatever else it was, the War on Poverty reflected an arrogance of power so typical of the United States in the early 1960s. Starting from John Kennedy's declaration that Americans would "bear any burden" and "pay any price," the nation embarked on a series of ventures that bespoke a conviction of limitless power at home as well as abroad. The war in Vietnam certainly fit that mold, as did the effort to put a man on the moon by the end of the decade. The War on Poverty fits here too. But policymakers and the public alike found technological goals easier to achieve than human improvement. The nation put an American on the moon but failed to keep one in Saigon, and found it increasingly difficult to guarantee the safety of Americans in their urban centers. Lyndon Johnson later lamented to Doris Kearns:

> I wish it had been different. I wish the public had seen the task of ending poverty the same way as they saw the task of getting to the moon, where they accepted mistakes as a part of the scientific process. I wish they had let us experiment with different programs, admitting that some were working better than others. It would have made everything easier. But I knew that the moment we said out loud that this or that program was a failure, then the wolves who never wanted us to be successful in the first place would be down upon us at once, tearing away at every joint, killing our effort before we even had a chance.

Structural changes in the economy also plagued the War on Poverty. Because prosperity continued throughout much of the sixties, the public often assumed that once discriminatory barriers were removed, minorities would be able to fend for themselves in the marketplace. But was this true? In the words of one economist, there were "simply an inadequate number of jobs at wages above the poverty level to absorb all job seekers." By the 1970s Americans would hear about the "rust belt," the disappearance of traditional manufacturing jobs which were never to return. This trend was already well under way in the sixties, and the entry of baby boomers into the work force exacerbated the adjustment problem. (Graduate school populations rose along with draft calls, postponing workforce entry for many, but this did not help the poor much in their search for long-term employment at good wages.) Economic growth, in short, was not the panacea promised in the 1964 tax cut. In his study of federal antipoverty programs, Robert Haveman stated the problem succinctly:

> In the mid-1960s, no major increase in income transfers to the poor, no system of demogrants, family allowances, or negative income taxes, and no other policy to alter directly the income distribution was proposed by the President or implemented by Congress. Nor was a major direct attack on structural weaknesses in the labor market proposed or implemented. Efforts to insure equal opportunity in employment form the only measure designed to increase the employment and earnings of the poor by explicitly increasing the demand for their services.

The administration offered, in the words of another analyst, a "service strategy when you had a structural diagnosis." This also meant that the War on Poverty rested as much on civil rights as it did on economics. And when civil rights idealism turned to racial divisiveness, the backlash spilled over to the antipoverty effort, producing a crisis for liberals that was highlighted by the Watts riots. How could their civil rights initiatives have been so successful and yet the problems persist? And because so many OEO programs targeted particular constituencies rather than broad job-creation efforts, they also fractured the coalition that comprised the Democratic party by setting civil rights and labor, blacks and whites, at each other's throats. Critics complained that the party represented "special interests" to the exclusion of the general public.

Conflict rather than consensus became a theme. As welfare rights activist George Wiley observed, "I am not at all convinced that comfortable, affluent, middle-class Americans are going to move over and share their wealth and resources with the people who have none." But the poor could seek leverage by organizing and exerting "their political muscle." They did so in 1967 with the formation of the National Welfare Rights Organization (NWRO). The NWRO had an impact. By the early 1970s the number of lawyers focusing on poverty issues had risen by 650 percent, and they appealed 164 cases to the Supreme Court. Welfare was now seen as less of a stigma and more of a "right," but the shift alienated much of the nonpoor public.

With all its initiatives, the War on Poverty nonetheless failed to address the larger issue of persistence. In 1967 SDS founder Alan Haber launched a withering critique of how an affluent society produced an "underclass." "They set up a re-inforcing situation: people are poor because they don't have money, and they don't have money because they are poor, and they stay both poor and without money because they don't have the political power to change their situation." That failure, the Southern Student Organizing Committee argued, permitted "local poverty programs to be run by whites who profited from poverty by owning slums, underpaying workers, gouging debtors, and the like."

The debate over the successes and failures of the War on Poverty continues even today, not only in order to reach a historical judgment on specific programs and on the Great Society as a whole, but also as a commentary on the viability of public social policy as a mechanism for change. Perhaps the major contribution of the War on Poverty is that it focused attention on a fundamental issue and argued that deliberate policymaking rather than casual economic growth was necessary if all citizens were to share in the promise of American life.

There are several pieces to this ongoing debate. One focuses on the motivation behind the War on Poverty. Some argue that black militancy as well as an effort to secure Democratic party hegemony drove decision-making. Frances Fox Piven and Richard Cloward, both of whom helped shape the policy as activists and theoreticians, make this argument, as does the historian Allen Matusow. Most of the War's architects disavow any such motive. Other analysts allow that Great Society policymakers meant well but complain that their goal exceeded their reach. Scholars and policymakers such as Sar Levitan, James Sundquist, and James Patterson fall into this camp. Some critics assert that, like most government programs, antipoverty efforts took on a life of their own and created a self-serving bureaucracy who became constituents of the program as much as the poor themselves.

Another argument concerns cost. Eliminating poverty is expensive, far more expensive than anyone imagined in 1964. While the Great Society released about six million Americans from the bonds of poverty between 1964 and 1969, it did so with ever-escalating bureaucratic and financial costs. Forty-five federal social programs spent $9.9 billion in 1961; eight years later 435 programs spent $25.6 billion. Yet the $1.5 billion authorized for the War on Poverty in 1966 represented only 1.5 percent of the total federal budget. OEO's annual expenditures between 1965 and 1968 averaged just $50 to $65 per year for each American in poverty, and much of that went to administrative costs. This amount paled in contrast to spending on the war in Vietnam, where by 1967 the United States was spending about $300,000 to kill one Viet Cong. Most people understood that foreign wars, popular or not, involved sacrifice. The War on Poverty, as it rode the crest of economic growth, promised to be cost-free; when the American public recognized that it might demand sacrifice, the program took on another dimension.

The third aspect of the debate over the War on Poverty is the most important for both history and contemporary policy. Did the War on Poverty succeed or fail? And, perhaps more central to the contending parties, did the War on Poverty as well as the Great Society as a whole produce or exacerbate social pathologies that have infected American political and social life since the sixties? The revival of ideology as an element of mainstream politics has driven much of this debate. During the 1980s a resurgent conservatism attacked Great Society efforts and embraced free-market capitalism as a chosen instrument for reform.

Probably the landmark studies in this debate are the works of George Gilder and Charles Murray. Gilder's *Wealth and Poverty* (1981) and *The Spirit of Enterprise* (1984) argued that public policies exacerbated individual deficiencies to cause poverty. Murray's 1984 book, *Losing Ground: American Social Policy, 1950–1980,* became especially controversial and widely popular among Reagan conservatives. Murray argued that the social policies of the Great Society, particularly its antipoverty program, represented a radical shift in government. The poverty program failed to ameliorate social and economic inequalities, and its financial costs proved to be prohibitive. "It amounted to a revolution," he concluded, and "altered a long-standing national consensus about what it means to be poor. . . ." LBJ's programs, he argued, interrupted a steady decline of poverty since 1950. When social program spending increased during the 1970s, poverty increased.

Murray complained that, beginning in 1964, social policy ignored several fundamental premises of American popular ideology: that incentives and disincentives drive individuals' behavior ("sticks and carrots work"); that in "the absence of countervailing influences, people will avoid work and be amoral"; and that people "must be held responsible for their actions" even though they may not ultimately be responsible for them.

But Murray's models, "Harold" and "Phyllis," resided in a state with abnormally high welfare benefits (Pennsylvania), and he ascribed all of the problems of the 1970s to 1960s legislation, without much evidence of a connection. This led him to claim that antipoverty programs contributed to poverty. He also used statistics selectively, omitting such factors as unemployment rates and the business cycle in his calculation of changing poverty rates. After 1973 the economy deteriorated, but Murray seemingly ignored that as a factor influencing poverty. Murray's conclusion also failed to recognize the continuing impact of racial discrimination in American life. In effect he demonized the Great Society, and the War on Poverty in particular, as well intentioned but misguided. They created, rather than eliminated, a culture of poverty, he argued, by changing the reward structure and encouraging deviant behavior.

The most significant response to Murray has come from William Julius Wilson, whose work *The Truly Disadvantaged: The Inner City, the Underclass, and Public Policy* appeared in 1987, three years after Murray's book. Wilson noted that sixties liberals rejected much of the culture-of-poverty theory, believing that limited opportunity produced ghetto-specific behavior. Thus Lyndon Johnson sought and got an Economic Opportunity Act from the Congress in 1964. Wilson argues that the real explanation of what happened since the sixties lies not in the culture-of-poverty theory but in long-term economic change and the idea of "social isolation. . . . Contact between groups of different classes and/or racial backgrounds is either lacking or has become increasingly intermittent. . . ."

This enhanced "the effects of living in a highly concentrated poverty area." These poor people are, as Wilson's title indicates, "truly disadvantaged."

The causes of this social isolation are varied. Daniel Patrick Moynihan and other social analysts outlined some of them in the mid-1960s, but the racial climate was such then that critics dismissed them as mere reflections of racial discrimination or a lack of opportunity, not as causes of poverty. In addition, many people (including some policymakers) had an essentially static view of poverty that established a fixed benchmark against which to measure progress. People's lives and environments, however, are dynamic rather than static.

The synergy of changing social conditions compounds the problem. When Moynihan studied black families in 1965, for instance, 25 percent of black births were illegitimate, and women headed nearly 25 percent of black families; by 1980 those figures had jumped to 57 percent and 43 percent, respectively. Studies of welfare benefits have found that the level of benefits is largely unrelated to the percentage of out-of-wedlock births, though critics constantly argue to the contrary. Similar studies have revealed that the absence of males in the household relates more to the lack of steady jobs than to welfare policies or to a moral distintegration among African Americans. The critics, in short, have too often ignored evidence to advance their own political agenda. As Wilson points out, President Reagan was "able to persuade the middle classes that the drop in their living standards was attributable to the poor (and implicitly, minorities), and that he could restore those standards with sweeping tax and budget cuts."

Despite his attacks on Murray and other critics of the War on Poverty, Wilson is no apologist for Great Society policies. He argues that their major flaw was the lack of job-creation policies to attack underemployment and unemployment and a misplaced emphasis on environmental factors and group rights rather than structural organization.

> Just as the architects of the War on Poverty failed to relate the problems of the poor to the broader processes of American economic organization, so too have the advocates for minority rights failed in significant numbers to understand that many contemporary problems of race, especially those that engulfed the minority poor, emanate from the broader problems of societal organization and therefore cannot be satisfactorily addressed by race-specific programs to eliminate racial discrimination and eradicate racial prejudices.

Analysts also confuse "historic discrimination" with "contemporary discrimination." The civil rights laws and equal-opportunity provisions of the 1964 and 1965 legislation addressed the former, but ongoing changes in the nation's economic structure exacerbate the latter. An Illinois study of plant closings in the 1970s, for instance, revealed that industrial relocation reduced black employment three times more than it did white employment.

Wilson's arguments point to one of the unfortunate liabilities of the Great Society: the coincidence of civil rights and other economic and social reforms. Too often, as noted earlier, the public associated the War on Poverty with civil rights efforts. By 1967 it was almost impossible to disentangle the two in the public mind. And not without reason. Growing urban problems, racial riots, rising black militancy, the move of the civil rights movement from the South to the North, whites' expectations that the end of legal discrimination would create opportunity for blacks—all produced a perception that antipoverty was a program for minorities. The early sixties vision of poor white coal miners in Appalachia, so evident in the Appalachia Aid Bill of 1965, gave way to the late sixties vision of the black poor in urban slums. Ironically, both suffered from structural economic change and a lack of good jobs—neither of which the War on Poverty directly addressed.

In assessing the failure or success of the War on Poverty, one must note that its failure to address the jobs question did not go unnoticed. The House Subcommittee on the War on Poverty Program concluded that a successful employment program was needed. The Kerner Commission on urban riots in 1967, the Poor People's Campaign of 1968, even the earlier 1963 March on Washington all focused on jobs as a central recommendation. How does one account for this failure? By focusing on services rather than employment, the antipoverty program hoped to avoid any direct threat to white jobholders. By emphasizing the individual problems of the poor it avoided broader issues of structural and institutional change that challenged the consensus head-on. LBJ remained convinced that economic growth would be an effective and painless cure for joblessness. Unfortunately, economic growth was not evenly distributed and largely bypassed weaker economic groups.

Finally, the broad focus on poverty disguised the experience of some of the particulars within that category. Many of the poor, for example, were elderly. Between 1966 and the early 1980s the government raised Social Security benefits on a regular basis, federalized welfare costs for the elderly, and tied benefit payments to the cost of living. As this occurred, the elderly emerged from poverty without any semblance of structural reform. The addition of Medicare and Medicaid in 1965 further alleviated problems of the elderly. In 1968 the poverty rate among those sixty-five and over in the United States was 28 percent; in 1996 it was 11 percent. Elsewhere the poverty rate for fully employed African Americans dropped from 43 percent in 1959 to 16 percent in 1979. This is success, but not one that stemmed solely from War on Poverty programs.

With all its warts and failures, the War on Poverty did clearly identify poverty and joblessness as the responsibility of the federal government. Americans came to realize that poverty and its causes were much more complex than they had believed in 1964. In the words of one antipoverty warrior who admitted their naiveté: "We assumed that, given enough attention, we really could do something. It's a far more intractable problem than we realized." Whether or not the American people and their political representatives had the will to tackle the causes of poverty was another question. In the short run the financial demands and psychic costs of the war in Vietnam curtailed such a commitment. In the long run, by the time the cold war with its defense spending demands had ended in the 1980s, a conservative backlash against the sixties and everything they purported to represent had set in. By then the national economy suffered from both internal decay and the external pressures of globalization, and personal incomes had remained essentially stagnant for more than two decades. The public mood was increasingly antigovernment. Since every president elected after Richard Nixon in 1972 had run against "Washington," the prospects for new or innovative national programs remained slim. Blaming current woes on past programs brought a greater political return than trying to forge a new public consensus to overcome poverty.

Overlooked by public and politicians alike was the fact that the number of poverty-stricken Americans had fallen from 18 percent (1960) to 9 percent (1972), despite the paucity of funding and the short-lived duration of the War on Poverty. Two decades later, however, in the absence of a continuing commitment, the situation had deteriorated. By 1996 the Children's

Defense Fund reported that 22 percent of children in the United States lived in poverty, with some urban rates exceeding 35 percent and rates among black children greater than 50 percent. In addition, 31 percent of young families *worked* at or below the poverty level. The failure painlessly and quickly to banish poverty from the United States, like so many other naive hopes punctured by sharp realities, created a legacy of cynicism that has only deepened with time.

3

Health and Education

THE CENTRAL PRINCIPLES of Lyndon Johnson's program for the Great Society were those of amelioration and opportunity. LBJ firmly believed that if the federal government could ameliorate the most oppressive disadvantages Americans suffered, and at the same time provide the opportunity for individuals to escape those disadvantages and improve their own lives, the United States would achieve a Great Society. Central to both was the concept of access—to the polls, to public services, to participation, and to health care and education.

Proposals for federal benefits to the medically indigent had surfaced periodically since the end of World War II. President Harry Truman tried to pass health care legislation in 1949 to cover persons of all ages, but a conservative Republican Congress defeated his efforts. Since then the American Medical Association had relentlessly attacked any federal medical programs as "socialized medicine." Even efforts to fluoridate drinking water in the early 1960s came under attack from conservative and right-wing groups, who claimed they were a Communist plot to poison Americans or to install listening devices in their teeth. Eventually, in most communities, health concerns overcame ideological and political objections, and fluoridated water (to help fight tooth decay) became a reality.

During the early 1960s, however, pressure mounted for a federal effort to bring medical care to the poor. In the late 1950s Rhode Island Democrat Aime Forand had introduced legislation to cover hospital and surgical costs under Social Security. Although backed by labor, the proposal failed to clear the House Ways and Means Committee and reach the floor of Congress. Arkansas Democrat Wilbur Mills, who chaired the committee, was a stubborn obstacle to any broad medical care legislation. In 1960 Congress enacted a limited measure, the Kerr-Mills Bill, which provided care to the "medically needy." Participation was not automatic; states had to join the program, and participants had to pass a means test. During the next few years the importance of medical care as a step along the path to opportunity found greater acceptance. By 1962 the federal government provided health services to Cuban refugees and to migrant farm workers, and by 1965 participants in Head Start and residents of Appalachia also received health care. The OEO's War on Poverty included the development of neighborhood health centers, though their ties to Community Action Programs made them controversial. In 1964 the federal government spent almost $8 billion for health and medical services to the poor, even in the absence of a comprehensive federal medical care program. Health care deficiencies of the poor remained alarming, however, and the delivery of services continued to be disorganized and inefficient. Efforts to pass remedial legislation in 1964 failed when a health care proposal again could not clear the House Ways and Means Committee.

The 1964 Democratic landslide changed the congressional situation, producing a clear majority in favor of medical care to the aged. To counter the continued opposition of the American Medical Association, President Johnson appointed a blue-ribbon panel of experts chaired by Michael DeBakey, a noted

Houston heart surgeon. The panel's report highlighted how limited was access to first-rate medical care in the United States. When Congress reconvened in 1965, the president immediately asked for action. He warned that "Unless we do better, two-thirds of all Americans now living will suffer or die from cancer, heart disease, or stroke: I expect you to do something about it." The solution, Johnson told Congress, was "to assure the availability of and accessibility to the best health care for all Americans regardless of age, geography, or economic status." What was needed was the right political mix to produce a bill that would pass. Introduced in the House by Democrat Cecil King of California, and into the Senate by New Mexico Democrat Clinton Anderson, the King-Anderson Bill (Medicare) became S. 1 and H.R. 1—the first order of business for the new Congress.

King set the tone for the ensuing debate when he told his fellow congressmen: "We can no longer permit hospital costs—or the fear of hospital costs—to deprive our elderly citizens of the security and peace of mind that should be their due after a lifetime of work." Health costs, King warned, were the "most serious remaining threat to financial security in old age," and were the "most important single reason for the continuing need for the aged to resort to public assistance." The King-Anderson Bill proposed a compulsory program covering all persons sixty-five and older, excepting only government workers and some aliens. Quickly dubbed "Medicare," it provided hospital care (60 days), posthospital care (60 days), home health care visits (240 days), and outpatient diagnostic services. (These benefits were later revised upward in the final bill.) Patients would pay some of the costs, but most expenses were to be financed through increased Social Security taxes. The measure would not cover medical and drug expenses incurred outside hospitals. The entire program would be administered through a separate trust fund within the Social Security system. Projected costs were $2 billion for the first full year of operation.

King-Anderson was not the only proposal to come before the Congress, however. The American Medical Association, knowing that it no longer had the votes to thwart any federal medical proposal, came forward with one of its own. The AMA measure was dubbed "eldercare." This was a benign-sounding label for a fully voluntary program available to individuals sixty-five and over *only* if the individual states agreed to sign up for it. Financed by federal-state matching funds and premiums from participants, it was projected to cost about $2 billion per year in federal and state funds. When Texas Senator John Tower touted the measure to his congressional colleagues, he focused on its central principle: "the doctors' program would offer free choice of physician and hospital—without Federal bureaucratic interference." Indeed, some state medical associations threatened to boycott any federal Medicare program.

"Eldercare," Tower insisted, would offer "better care than medicare." The King-Anderson proposal, he argued, was dangerously expensive—"medicare can destroy Social Security as we know it." Few agreed with him. Liberals, such as Ohio's Stephen Young, attacked the AMA plan: "They term their proposal 'eldercare.' In reality, it is a 'don't care' program insofar as the elderly of this Nation are concerned. 'Elder scare' would also be an appropriate name for their bill." New Jersey Representative Frank Thompson was more sarcastic, proposing "Doctorcare." This was to "be financed by a two-per-cent federal tax on applesauce, and the funds were to be used to provide special therapy for any physician who felt himself suffering from an urge to make house calls; if he didn't respond satisfactorily to the arguments of his colleagues over the phone, he would be rushed to the nearest Cadillac showroom."

Many Republicans objected to Medicare but did not believe that eldercare was sufficient. They backed an alternative introduced by Wisconsin Republican John Byrnes, the ranking minority member of the House Ways and Means Committee. Byrnes proposed a standard indemnity plan, similar to one available to federal employees, to pay doctor and hospital bills. It provided for voluntary participation but was administered by the federal government and financed by individual premiums on a sliding scale according to ability to pay. States and the federal government would also contribute, and estimated costs were $3.4 billion per year. Most significant about the Byrnes Bill was that it proposed to cover physicians' services and drugs, neither of which were covered by the King-Anderson or eldercare plans.

Hearings on the proposed legislation were often turbulent. The insurance industry warned that federal health care meant the end of the private insurance industry and opposed the provision of health care benefits to the elderly "irrespective of their ability to finance their own health care costs." There was, said one spokesman, "little or no necessary social purpose" to such a program. The American Medical Association opposed federal "interference" in health care and claimed it would lead to overutilization of health benefits and rising costs, which in turn would provide an incentive to substitute cost for quality as a control mechanism. (This turned out to be what happened.) Other medical specialists chimed in, but their testimony was often paradoxical. They opposed federal health care as unnecessary, even as they objected that the proposed plan excluded their particular specialty. The pharmaceutical industry, for instance, complained that specifying certain drugs to be covered was discriminatory, and chiropractors worried that they were not covered even though forty-seven states legally recognized their profession.

Although the three measures seemed mutually exclusive, and in fact were introduced with that intent, Wilbur Mills used his control of the Ways and Means Committee to effectively combine the King-Anderson and Byrnes proposals into one bill. The result was two amendments to the Social Security Act. Title 18 (Medicare) covered everyone over age sixty-five and was divided into two parts. Part A was a hospital insurance program, a revision of King-Anderson. It was compulsory in the sense that while one could refuse its benefits, one could not refuse to participate in it. Funding came from a small payroll tax and participants' premiums. Part B provided for a voluntary insurance program to pay doctors' bills (part of the Byrnes proposal) and created a federally subsidized Supplementary Medical Insurance for doctors' bills and drugs.

Title 19 (Medicaid) offered liberalized medical care for the "medically needy," in effect an extension of the existing Kerr-Mills program. It targeted low-income individuals regardless of age who were already participating in other welfare programs. Medicaid hoped to use federal funds to help states provide comprehensive medical care to the needy (families with dependent children, the elderly, and blind and disabled persons). A range of public and private providers would deliver these services and would receive reimbursement from the states. The system was to work much like private insurance programs and bring middle-class medical benefits to those in need.

Although a majority of Republicans and Southern Democrats opposed the health care measure, the final bill proved a smashing political success. The revised legislation, which also provided for a 7 percent raise in Social Security benefits, sailed through both the House (307 to 116) and Senate (70 to 24) in the summer of 1965. A $5,000 per day lobbying campaign by the AMA, which eventually spent $50 million, failed to derail the measure.

President Lyndon Johnson signed the Medicare Bill on July 30, 1965, with implementation to begin July 1, 1966. The ceremony was held in Harry Truman's hometown of Independence, Missouri, to honor Truman's earlier efforts to pass federal medical care legislation. Following the signing, the president spoke about how the measure advanced his vision of the Great Society:

> No longer will older Americans be denied the healing miracle of modern medicine. No longer will illness crush and destroy the savings that they have so carefully put away over a lifetime so that they might enjoy dignity in their later years. No longer will young families see their own incomes, and their own hopes, eaten away simply because they are carrying out their deep moral obligations to their parents, and to their uncles, and their aunts.

In defeat, the AMA did not immediately embrace the new program. At its June meeting the AMA's house of delegates voted to allow individual physicians to decide whether or not to boycott Medicare. Eight states had already passed resolutions supporting a boycott. But by October the AMA was ready to give in, and its house of delegates voted not to boycott the new program in the face of advice that such a move would be a restraint of trade and likely violate the Sherman Anti-Trust Act.

From the outset Medicare was an extremely popular program. Since everyone eligible for Social Security was eligible for Medicare, the program benefited the middle class and the wealthy as well as the poor. Not surprisingly, therefore, polls indicated overwhelming public support: 85 percent in New

York, 82 percent in Pennsylvania, 74 percent in North Carolina, and 73 percent in Michigan supported additional Social Security taxes to pay for the measure. That popularity was quickly evident in the participation rates: 93 percent of all senior citizens enrolled in the voluntary Part B program. Much like the antipoverty program, Medicare uncovered a vast wasteland where Americans hungered for affordable medical care. Before its passage a fifth of all Americans living in poverty, including many elderly, had never been examined by a physician.

The problem with Medicare was that it effected reform without making significant structural change. Although it was advanced as an insurance measure, most of the elderly seized upon it as an instrument to deliver health care services. In addition, neither Medicare nor Medicaid significantly changed the structure of health care in the country. Federal supervision was minimal, and the private sector (hospitals and doctors) chose insurance companies such as Blue Cross as their fiscal intermediaries. Both the processing of claims as well as the payment rates were structured to reflect those in the private sector, and participants could freely choose their own doctors. As one study of the issue noted: "Medicare thus began with an apparent paradox. Private enterprise had failed, markedly, to provide adequate health insurance for the elderly: hence the passage of Medicare. Yet private insurance was chosen to administer the new governmental system." Although its opponents tried to demonize Medicare as "socialism," it was scarcely that. It owned no hospitals, employed no physicians. Indeed, it failed to confront the question of whether or not Americans had a basic right to health services.

Cost control was totally absent from both programs. This was no accident. Wilbur Cohen, undersecretary of health, education and welfare, had to assure Congress that "there would be no real controls over hospitals or physicians." Cohen proposed raising the earnings base for Social Security taxes to produce funds to pay for the program. In that way it would not impact lower-income workers since they already paid the maximum Social Security tax. But the emphasis at the outset of the programs was on access to medical care for more individuals within the mainstream of American medicine, not cost containment. Moreover, unlike Social Security in the 1930s, this legislation did not determine eligibility through a period of payroll tax deductions.

Ironically, those who most strongly opposed the program turned out to be among its chief beneficiaries. Payments according to the traditional fee-for-service basis caused physicians' incomes to rise about 11 percent per year on average during the first seven years of the program. Hospitals were also allowed to bill on a cost basis without any controls on the appropriateness of the services provided. Medicaid was even more open-ended in terms of expense. Even though it was categorical, based on welfare classifications, Medicaid was state administered. This meant that it was not standardized throughout the country with respect to the services provided or the level of income that determined eligibility. Indeed, there were fifty-six separate programs, each with a different set of eligibility rules. This lack of consistency created financial and political controversy.

Further difficulty was caused by the redefinition of federal and state roles under the Medicare and Medicaid programs. In this respect they resembled the antipoverty program, which sought to create new relationships between local, state, and federal entities to solve broad social problems. In each instance the issue was the allocation of power and authority between state and federal officials, particularly concerning fiscal responsibility and financial resources. John Gardner, HEW secretary, spoke to the new federal-state relationship envisioned with the health care program.

> That may be the most revolutionary single thing that we are doing today. It means that the Federal Government, far from trying to dominate, is trying increasingly to preserve the pluralism of our society. We are heading toward a new kind of creative federalism, toward the establishment of new relationships that will see us through not only the complexity of today but the increasing complexity of the decades to come.

Federal expenditures on health services and facilities, $2.9 billion in 1959–1960, rose to $20.6 billion in 1970–1971. Where only about 25 percent of health expenditures in 1960 were publicly financed (largely for military personnel), by 1969 almost 40 percent came from public programs. More important was the cost-shifting that occurred. Although institutionalized patient charges rose by a third from 1965 to 1967, individuals' out-of-pocket costs declined by 15 percent thanks to Medicare. As one study of the program argued, what drove costs upward more than participation was the formula itself. This allowed hospitals to be paid 2 percent more than their costs in order to finance hospital expansion, and therefore offered no incentive to cut those costs. In addition, Medicare paid hospitals and doctors to treat indigent patients they had once treated at reduced or no cost; and reimbursement guidelines for physicians relied on "customary charges" that were often high. As Sar Levitan and Robert Taggart concluded, the "scapegoats for this unexpected growth were 'greedy' doctors and 'hypochondriac' beneficiaries."

The new medical care program, with its emphasis on access and opportunity, drew sustenance from recently passed civil rights measures. Wilbur Cohen highlighted the connection.

"On the day before Medicare went into effect," he noted, "in every hospital in the South, over every drinking fountain, over every bathroom, over every cafeteria, there were signs reading 'White' and 'Colored' for separate but presumably equal facilities. On the day that Medicare went into effect in the South, all those signs and separate facilities began to come down." Progress along this line was often glacial, but change did occur as the federal government enforced Title VI of the Civil Rights Act, which banned racial discrimination in federally assisted programs. Between 1966 and 1969 the number of minority patients in hospitals increased by 30 percent, and 61 percent more hospitals could count minority doctors or dentists on their staffs. Cost projections were inadequate because they had failed to recognize the "dismal state of medical care for the poor as well as the growth factors built into the program." The number of persons receiving Medicaid benefits increased nearly 17 percent annually between 1967 and 1973, as welfare rolls climbed during this same period. The parallel with the antipoverty program was instructive. The road to the Great Society was longer and bumpier than Lyndon Johnson had envisioned.

Events later proved, as the historian Allen Matusow has argued, that Medicare was a "ruinous accommodation between reformers and vested interests." But in the context of 1965 there was no politically feasible alternative. Any effort to alter the delivery system for health care in the United States, or change the way in which health care was financed, faced certain defeat. Twenty years later Wilbur Cohen recalled that "it wasn't possible in 1965 to put cost controls in it. It would have never passed Congress. That would have been federal control, which was the whole political issue at that time. Even if we could have, no one knew how to do it in 1965." In fact health care costs were rising rapidly even before the passage of

Medicare. Between 1950 and 1963 the average daily cost of a hospital stay rose 149 percent while the cost of living increased only 27 percent. After passage of Medicare both indices continued to climb. From 1965 to 1986 the Consumer Price Index (CPI) increased 350 percent, but the medical portion of that index rose 484 percent! Still, as Theodore Marmor and others have pointed out, medical prices rose faster in relation to the CPI *before* passage of Medicare than after.

Critics' claims that Medicare was socialistic missed the mark almost entirely. While Title 18 did cover elderly individuals without regard to ability to pay, Medicare worked through the private sector in its utilization of doctors and hospitals. And the private sector was interested in profit, not cost containment. As Cohen reminded critics a decade later, those "who long for perfect legislation in the American environment do not recognize the imagination, creativity, genius, and conspiracy which exists in the mind and heart of one or two percent of our adult population." In addition, as Edward Berkowitz noted in his biography of Cohen, in 1965 few people believed that medical plans of this sort led to inflation. "The preoccupation with inflation," Berkowitz observed, "was largely a post-1965 phenomenon; only in retrospect would Medicare appear to be flawed." The later shift in emphasis from the provision of services to managerial efficiency, together with a declining national economy, an inflationary spiral, and a significant rise in antigovernment feeling, led to attacks on federal medical programs as part of a wasteful welfare bureaucracy.

Within a decade after the passage of Medicare, policy studies assessed the federal effort. One by Karen Davis typified the results. Davis noted that both Medicare and Medicaid had reduced financial barriers to medical care in the United States, and in the process had markedly improved the use of medical services by the poor and the elderly. Although the poor had benefited, they still largely frequented public clinics and non-specialists, and did not yet participate in "mainstream medicine." Nor did Medicare guarantee the elderly equal access to medical facilities regardless of income. The programs had alleviated, but not eliminated, the financial hardships imposed by medical bills on low-income families. Comprehensive health centers had delivered quality medicine, but where states retained widespread discretion, health care programs had not performed well. Finally, neighborhood health centers had improved access to medical care for rural residents and minorities, but both still faced nonfinancial barriers to quality medical care. In short, despite some problems, Medicare and Medicaid had only begun to address its two major objectives: providing adequate medical care to the elderly and poor and alleviating the financial burden of medical care to low-income individuals and families.

Led by conservatives such as California Governor Ronald Reagan, attacks on Medicaid escalated by 1967, and the focus shifted from an emphasis on providing medical care to controlling welfare costs. With that shift, the possibility that either Congress or the public at large would address the question of access to medical care as a basic right all but disappeared. The opportunity for reform seemed to have passed, and the language of the debate became punitive rather than permissive. Reagan announced that, because of spiraling costs, he would cut Medicaid benefits in California to deal with a projected deficit of $71 million. Although by the spring of 1968 that "deficit" had become a surplus of $31 million, conservative opposition remained strong.

Meanwhile Congress passed the 1967 Social Security Amendments to deal with the Medicare and Medicaid deficits. Although often technical in nature, those amend-

ments deserve attention because they demonstrate both the
strengths and the weaknesses of the Great Society by 1967.
They reflected the paradoxical, even contradictory nature of
reform in the late sixties.

By 1967 President Johnson had urged an increase in Social
Security benefits for more than a year, with a target of a 10
percent increase in benefits coupled with a marginal increase
in Social Security taxes. House Republicans favored something less, closer to an 8 percent increase with no additional
taxes. LBJ viewed the increase as part of his antipoverty program and argued that a 15 percent rise in benefits would move
1.4 million persons out of poverty. Coupled with this was a
proposal to expand Medicare coverage to 1.5 million disabled
Americans who were under age sixty-five, in addition to improved public assistance programs at the state level. Billed as
the "most sweeping program for older Americans ever recommended by a United States President," these measures were
designed to use a popular program (Social Security) to advance ones less popular (antipoverty and Medicare) in Congress.

But Congress was wary, even though HEW Secretary John
Gardner testified that more than five million Social Security
beneficiaries "still live in poverty." House hearings raised the
question of financing Social Security through general revenue
funds, reflecting a fear that payroll tax limits had been
reached. Much of the testimony focused on the escalating costs
of medical care in the United States. Even administration witnesses admitted that costs were well above earlier estimates.
The House reacted by including a mandatory work-training
provision for AFDC recipients, even mothers of small children, and by cutting back federal commitments to Medicaid.
Labor leader George Meany of the AFL-CIO urged Congress
to increase Medicare and Medicaid benefits by at least 20 per-

cent, which he viewed as a "down payment" on an eventual 50 percent benefits increase. He also strongly opposed an effort to limit participation in the Medicaid program and urged that prescription drugs be covered under Medicare.

Opposition came from the U.S. Chamber of Commerce and the American Medical Association. Chamber spokesmen supported the Republican proposal of an 8 percent increase without new taxes, and criticized the administration's bill because it mixed "welfare concepts of need" with Social Security. The AMA opposed any form of federal medical care, arguing that it was not "in the public interest" and unnecessarily involved the federal government in the private sector. Expansion would increase the cost of health care, and the AMA strongly opposed providing benefits to the 1.5 million disabled Americans under age sixty-five. The doctors preferred a voluntary plan to replace Medicaid, one that would allow individuals to purchase private health insurance; at the same time the AMA favored full federal reimbursement of all drug costs under Medicare!

A final pocket of opposition came from the National Welfare Rights Organization. During the Senate hearings a group of African-American mothers staged a noisy demonstration at the witness table in opposition to tighter welfare provisions in the bill. One mother complained that the only time Congress ever listened was "when the cities are burning and the people are dying." But chairman Russell Long dismissed the women as "brood mares" and urged them to get jobs rather than sit in the hearing room. House Democrat Wilbur Mills later remarked, "You would think that the American way of life was built on a dole system to hear some people talk."

The bill reported out by the Ways and Means Committee rejected several key administration requests. Gone was the proposal to include in Medicare 1.5 million disabled persons under age sixty-five who received Social Security benefits. Gone also were provisions for greater coordination of state health planning, special minimum benefits for workers, Social Security coverage for 500,000 farm workers, pilot dental programs for children from low-income families, and a variety of other proposals. When the bill reached the House floor it did so under a closed rule prohibiting amendments from the floor. The earlier architect of Medicare, Representative Mills, reflected the changed congressional tone when he defended the changes by asking if it was "in the public interest for welfare to become a way of life?" The bill passed 416 to 3.

The Senate was more receptive to administration pleas for change, but a series of amendments from the floor increased the cost of the measure to almost $7 billion, virtually ensuring either a standoff in conference with the House version or a Senate capitulation. Particularly important was the Senate adoption of an amendment offered by Democrat Russell Long of Louisiana which would have forced the government to reduce the cost of drugs purchased under federal programs. Long argued that the cost of these drugs was artificially inflated, and the Senate passed the amended measure 78 to 6. But when the bill went to conference, almost every Senate amendment (including the Long Amendment) was removed from the final bill. Liberal senators, led by Democrats Robert Kennedy of New York and Fred Harris of Oklahoma, were so outraged by the Senate's concessions that they threatened a filibuster. Adroit parliamentary maneuvering by Long avoided the filibuster and secured Senate passage of the conference version. The final bill passed both the House and Senate by wide margins in mid-December. On January 2, 1968, President Johnson signed the measure.

As passed, the Social Security Amendments of 1967 were important both for what they did and did not do. First, the bill provided for an across-the-board 13 percent increase in Social Security benefits, to be paid for by raising both the Social Security tax rate and the wage base on which it rested. This piece of the bill promised to remove even more of the elderly from poverty and continue the transformation of Social Security from an old-age assistance program to an antipoverty program. At the same time, however, this increase extended to all Social Security recipients, not just the impoverished. Its impact, therefore, was to accelerate the financial drain on the Social Security system by middle- and upper-income elderly Americans. At the time few seemed to worry that it might endanger the financial health of the system itself.

The other three major sections of the bill dealt with Medicare, Medicaid, and welfare. The Medicare changes were largely permissive. They liberalized the payment options for medical reimbursement and included extended-care facilities and other services not previously covered. Patients or doctors could now submit itemized bills directly for reimbursement, even before the bill had been paid. "Reasonable" charges would be allowed for radiological and pathological services, physical therapy, diagnostic x-rays, and podiatrist care. Finally, the Department of Health, Education and Welfare was required to study the reimbursement costs for prescription drugs and devise a plan to control those costs.

Medicaid changes were both permissive and punitive. The bill limited the participation of the federal government in the program by stipulating that it would not provide matching funds to any state that allowed participants to earn more than 150 percent of the state's assistance income standard. This mild cost-containment effort promised to save $329 million in 1969 alone, and represented a small effort to curb Medicaid's growth among middle-class Americans and limit it to the needy as originally intended. At the same time, however, the bill increased the federal contribution toward the cost of medical personnel working in state Medicaid programs from 50 to 75 percent, and permitted Medicaid recipients to be reimbursed directly for physicians' and dentists' expenses they incurred. The other major portion of the legislation required states to monitor their Medicaid programs to ensure against unnecessary services or excessive costs.

The most punitive aspect of the bill was the public welfare section, though even this portion increased some benefits. The legislation required work-training for AFDC recipients and provided for the creation of day-care centers for children whose mothers were in training or had found a job. Federal matching funds were restricted to the children of unemployed fathers rather than mothers. Yet the measure also increased funds for child welfare and authorized use of the Internal Revenue Service to track down runaway parents of children receiving AFDC. The AFDC provisions represented an effort to curb the sudden growth of AFDC rolls, which had doubled in the preceding ten years. The Johnson administration had requested almost none of these provisions.

The 1967 Social Security Amendments began a trend that accelerated with each new year—a determination to focus on cost containment rather than on national health care. Also in 1967, congressional discussions to restrict welfare dwarfed debates over medical care. At the same time Americans were becoming more and more health-conscious, health care technology was entering a new (and much more expensive) age, and the demand for health care was outstripping all predictions. The result was a steady escalation in health care costs, which further encouraged a cautious and increasingly conservative Congress to avoid the national health care issue.

What produced this turnabout? In their detailed study of

Medicare and Medicaid, Robert and Rosemary Stevens argued that it was never a health care *system* at all. At best, they wrote, both health and welfare were a "patchwork of programs developed at different times for different needs and different groups." Although initiated by the federal government, Medicaid was run by the states and varied statewide across the country. Federal-state coordination was inefficient and uneven, with growing incidence of fraud. Medical providers pushed up their fees, and even racketeering was widespread as doctors reported phantom patient visits in order to receive federal reimbursement funds. In 1970 the government reported that more than 30 percent of all doctors who had received large Medicaid payments had cheated on their taxes. When physicians' earnings rose rapidly, therefore, the public (not always incorrectly) blamed excessive federal medical reimbursements. Eligibility levels also remained uneven. The 1967 Social Security Amendments perpetuated this by further defining the "medically needy" (those eligible for Medicaid) in welfare terms. Even in 1970, twenty-three states still had no programs for the "medically indigent" (low-income persons, not on Medicaid, whose large medical bills qualified them for support).

In a 1968 report, the Department of Health, Education and Welfare noted that 45 million Americans remained in the low-income bracket. The "underlying assumption" was that their needs should be met. This helped fuel the rising cost spiral of medical care, in part because the extent of those needs remained unknown. Health care expenditures for the poor jumped from $1.6 billion in 1966 to $5.1 billion in 1968. This led to demands for more federal control, if only to limit costs, which in turn excited critics of federal power to attack the entire program with increased vigor. Ironically, many people entitled to participate in these programs remained ignorant of them. More than 70 percent of the "medically indigent" did not know they were entitled to Medicaid.

Because the public increasingly linked Medicaid to welfare, the growing backlash against welfare stimulated public opposition to Medicaid. Critics often claimed that the solution to welfare, reflected in the 1967 amendments, was to force recipients back into the work force and thereby reduce poverty. That would also curb the number of Medicaid recipients and contain the costs of the program. Retrenchment rather than expansion was the order of the day. Finally, as the historian Edward Berkowitz noted, the 1967 Social Security Amendments provided a snapshot of late-sixties politics and the disruption of the liberal coalition:

> Liberals, who strongly favored some features of the bill such as increased Social Security benefits and the notion of allowing welfare beneficiaries to keep some of their earnings, nonetheless perceived the measure as anticity and antiblack. Organized labor leaders and liberals joined in the cause of opposing higher Social Security taxes although for different reasons. Labor leaders worried about maintaining the income of the working man; liberals regarded higher Social Security taxes as a disguised way of financing the Vietnam War, and thus the unlikely vehicle of a Social Security bill became a means for them to express their opposition to that war. Conservatives, who very much wanted to contain welfare benefits, could not overlook the liberal features of the law. Hence, the bill, the very sort of bill that would have been inordinately popular a few years before, stirred up controversy.

The debate over federal aid to education proved to be less complex. Lyndon Johnson believed that access to quality education was the gateway to opportunity, the "guardian genius of our democracy." Johnson's commitment was a personal one that recalled his early days as a schoolteacher for impoverished Mexican-American youth in south Texas. Although the president repeatedly romanticized this early experience, it clearly shaped his vision of educational opportunity as a great equalizer. For many reformers, too, education was the great panacea. It would lead to better jobs, help children of the poor escape poverty forever, broaden the middle class, enrich personal lives, and turn the ladder of upward mobility into a fast-moving escalator.

Schools around the country in the mid-sixties were desperate for financial help. The leading edge of the postwar baby boom had reached them in the late 1950s, and by the mid-1960s this demographic revolution threatened to overwhelm local resources. Growing concerns about the impact of automation and new technologies led to calls for extended education. Education through and beyond high school seemed essential for the future, which meant that access must be improved and facilities expanded. Education became not only an expectation but a "right." The Soviets' launch of the Sputnik satellite in 1957 had created a sense of alarm that the United States was falling behind the Russians, at least in matters of science, in no small part because the American educational system was inadequate. Educators and government officials urged school districts to revise and toughen their curricula, particularly in the sciences. Especially with passage of the National Defense Education Act in 1958, educational needs became more closely linked to national policies and priorities.

But there remained the larger philosophical issue and political question of federal aid to education. Was it constitutional? Could parochial and private schools participate as well as public schools? Was it wise? Would not federal aid to education lead to federal control of education? Since World War II there had been federal aid to education, but it had been indirect or disguised. The GI Bill of Rights had provided the means for returning servicemen to continue their education, often enabling men who had only dreamed of higher education to receive a college degree. In the 1950s the federal government had made funds available for low-cost loans to build dormitories on college campuses throughout the country. Federal monies had also gone to local school districts under the impacted areas program. Tied to national defense, this helped offset the impact of federal employees' children on local schools, usually those adjacent to federal bases or installations. By 1960 polls consistently showed that 75 percent or more of the American public favored outright federal aid to education.

Efforts to implement such aid during the Kennedy administration, however, failed. Proposals ran afoul of the church-state controversy, compounded by the fact that a Catholic in the White House was sensitive to the issue of aid to parochial schools. With anti-Catholic rumors circulating that the Statue of Liberty was about to be renamed Our Lady of the Harbor, John Kennedy wished to avoid any hint that administration policies would privilege Catholics. More important, the major lobbying interests remained intransigent. The National Education Association and the National Council of Churches vehemently opposed federal aid to parochial schools. The National Catholic Welfare Conference, on the other hand, militantly insisted that parochial schools must participate or no one would. Together they killed all legislation. Yet the controversy proved instructive, because both public and parochial school interests learned that only through compromise would any legislation pass Congress. LBJ refused to forward federal aid to education legislation to the Congress until both the National Education Association and the National Catholic Welfare Conference agreed to support it.

John Gardner, president of the Carnegie Corporation, headed the Johnson task force concerned with education. With Francis Keppel, appointed commissioner of education under President Kennedy, and Wilbur Cohen, the task force reported to LBJ just after the November 1964 elections. It urged an overhaul of the American educational system to provide greater access for all. Barriers to access, such as impoverished school districts, insufficient special education resources, individual poverty that blocked education beyond the secondary level, and the educational ills of the nation's urban school districts, had to fall. Only by increasing the federal share of educational expenses, and thereby relieving the states and local school districts, could significant change be achieved.

The question was how this might be done without once again running afoul of the church-state issue. As conceived by Wilbur Cohen, the answer was to tie federal aid to students rather than to schools. This became known as the "child-benefit theory" and represented a significant breakthrough at the federal level. A similar approach had sometimes been used in earlier state legislation. And the Economic Opportunity Act of 1963 had provided educational aid to individuals based on their income rather than on the types of schools they attended. Together with the determination of public and parochial school interests to cooperate and fashion a bill that would pass Congress, the child-benefit approach led to landmark legislation in 1965.

That legislation was the Elementary and Secondary Education Act. Sent to Congress as the new year began, the proposal initially attracted support because it promised children of the poor an opportunity to break the shackles of poverty by developing their minds. HEW Secretary Anthony Celebrezze highlighted that theme in his testimony during House hearings. "The lack of adequate education for millions of our poorest young people," he asserted, "is a major factor in our present high rates of youth unemployment, delinquency, and crime." To further emphasize this link, Celebrezze noted that in the past decade "jobs for high school graduates have increased by 40 percent, jobs for those who failed to enter or finish high school have dropped by 10 percent." Mrs. Marion Street, president of the teachers' association in Philadelphia, sounded a related theme: "You will meet children from homes dilapidated, cold, and rundown, and visit with them in schools where plaster drops from the ceiling; broke windows go unfixed; adequate toilet facilities are nonexistent; and broken and faulty heaters endanger their health."

When the House debated the bill that spring, however, its members focused chiefly on the propriety of federal aid. While Republican Clarence Brown, Jr., of Ohio complained that the "bill is one of the most dangerous measures that has come before us in my time," a fellow Republican, John Anderson of Illinois, put the central question succinctly: "This is a very fundamental debate between those who think education is simply not a Federal function and those who do; between those who think it is something that constitutionally, historically, and traditionally has been reserved to the States and those who think otherwise." New York Republican Charles Goodell was more critical. Casting aside notions that this was a poverty program, Goodell asserted that its "true purpose" was to "authorize general aid without regard to need, and the clear intent is to radically change our historic structure of education by a dramatic shift of power to the Federal level." Paul Findley of Illinois denounced the measure as a "fateful first step" in this shift of power that would inevitably lead to federal authority "over what is taught in schools across this land." Virginia Democrat Howard Smith warned that "we apparently have come to the end of the road so far as local control over our education in public facilities is concerned." Despite this opposition, supporters of the bill, under the leadership of Georgia Democrat Phil Landrum, defeated almost all amendments and in effect limited debate. On March 26, 1965, with most Republicans and Southern Democrats opposed, the House passed the measure 263 to 153 and sent it on to the Senate. Although only 27 percent of House Republicans supported the bill, every one of the forty-eight Democrats elected in 1964 to replace a Republican voted for it.

Two weeks of hearings by the Senate Education Subcommittee produced few new arguments or evidence. Perhaps the most significant was the testimony of Dr. Benjamin Willis, superintendent of the Chicago schools. Willis not only articulated the widely supported argument that education was fundamental to attack poverty and provide opportunity, he summarized the major educational problems facing the nation's urban areas.

(1) Well-educated and highly skilled people are moving out of the city. (2) Their places are being taken by large families from the rural South. (3) In the midst of rapidly developing technological advances, the adults among the newcomers have little education and limited vocational skills. (4) The children, retarded in academic achievement and lacking in motivation for school, require specialized programs of education if they are to overcome the disadvantages imposed upon them by their limited backgrounds. (5) Programs to meet the needs of disadvantaged children have been successfully demonstrated in each of the great cities but these cannot be extended to serve all of the children in need because of lack of financial resources. (6) Local support of education comes largely from taxes on property; 12 cities pay well over 60 percent of the cost of operating their schools from local taxes. (7) By 1965 enrollments in the schools of

the great cities will have increased 48.6 percent over 1950, and these enrollments include large numbers of pupils requiring costly specialized programs. (8) Site and construction costs are considerably higher in the large cities than in smaller communities. (9) A large portion of the tax dollar in the great cities is required for nonschool governmental services. (10) In the face of increased need for financial resources, there is a smaller assessable tax base behind each child in the schools in the great cities than ever before. (11) The sharing of taxes from other sources and from other levels of government is required in order for the great cities to provide opportunities for their children, each in accordance with his need.

For most senators, the solution was more money. Federal aid would be added to state and local funds to improve educational opportunity. But New York Senator Robert Kennedy warned that the money would not likely be well spent, and that the school districts themselves were barriers to change. His brother, Senator Edward Kennedy of Massachusetts, complained simply that the funding was inadequate. Once the budget became "more flexible and revenue more available," he hoped that budgetary allocations could increase and more closely meet needs. (Indeed, federal funds to support elementary and secondary education nearly tripled from 1965 to 1966.) Edward Kennedy also suggested the creation of an American Teacher Corps, modeled on the Peace Corps, to send teachers into impoverished rural and urban areas for one or two years. This later became Title V of the Higher Education Act. Most other witnesses linked the lack of educational opportunity and poor academic performance to poverty. When the measure reached the Senate floor, under the leadership of Oregon Democrat Wayne Morse, three days of debate rejected all amendments, and the bill passed 73 to 18. Lyndon

Johnson flew to his former one-room schoolhouse in Stonewall, Texas, to sign the Elementary and Secondary Education Act (ESEA) on April 11, 1965.

The heart of the act was Title I. In keeping with the child-benefit theory, it provided for aid to poor children in slums and rural areas through an allocation formula. Funds were to be provided to the states based on each state's average expenditures per schoolchild, multiplied by the number of students from low-income families. This formula belied arguments that Title I was chiefly directed toward poor children and impoverished districts, because it rewarded wealthier states that already spent heavily on education. Indeed, later studies showed that while 81 percent of the poor children were concentrated in only 32 percent of the nation's school districts, school districts in almost 95 percent of the country's counties received federal aid. Oregon Democrat Edith Green's efforts to change this to a flat grant per poor child had met defeat in the House.

The act's other provisions were less controversial. Title II created a five-year program for school libraries to buy textbooks and other instructional materials. Title III established a five-year program of grants to the states to create supplemental educational centers and services. It focused on innovation rather than the support of existing programs. Opponents of these two sections charged that government funding of educational materials endangered local control. Yet they paralleled a major trend evident in both the civil rights and antipoverty legislation of the preceding year. They represented a nationalizing of citizenship, resting on a belief that American citizenship itself should bring certain rights and opportunities irrespective of where one resided.

Titles IV and V provided aid indirectly to schools through federal funds for educational research and strengthened state departments of education. Title VI addressed the issue of federal control by providing that no federal official "could exercise supervision over the curriculum, administration, or personnel of any institution or school system or over the selection of any instructional materials." In the end, money talked loud enough to quiet many ESEA critics.

Many of these issues simmered throughout the year, as the new education act did not take effect immediately. Congress took several months to vote funding for the measure, and the money did not reach some areas until April 1966, almost a year after the president signed the measure. Since this was near the end of a school year, its effects were delayed several months more, to the start of a new year. Perhaps more important, during the interval between the bill's passage and its implementation the political mood of the country changed dramatically. By the fall of 1966 LBJ's consensus was fading fast, as evidenced by Republican gains in the fall elections, several race riots, the turbulent experience of the civil rights movement as it moved out of the South and into the North, and the steadily rising opposition to American policies in Vietnam.

One of the most dramatic and controversial aspects of ESEA was its link to Title VI of the 1964 Civil Rights Act— the section that prohibited discrimination in any program that received federal funds. Passage of ESEA, especially its Title I provisions, provided the momentum to fulfill the promises of the Supreme Court's 1954 *Brown* decision on public school desegregation. The intervening decade had seen glacial progress, but Southern states now moved to integrate more quickly so as not to lose federal funding under the new legislation. This was not accomplished without tension. As one study noted, the Office of Education had to "induce instant desegregation and to end programmatic discrimination in every school district slated for the award of Federal aid. The price of failure would be the sacrifice of the very programs . . . which could attack the conditions that had created, stimulated, and maintained segregation and discrimination." By August 1965 more than nine hundred desegregation plans were pending.

Two situations dramatized the problem. In the South, although the number of black children in desegregated schools throughout the old Confederacy had tripled in the year following passage of the Civil Rights Act, by 1965–1966 and the passage of ESEA about 94 percent of those children remained in segregated schools. Throughout the South and border states as a whole, only 16 percent of black children attended desegregated schools. Education Commissioner Francis Keppel withheld funds from more than sixty school districts throughout the South for probable noncompliance with Title VI.

In some Northern cities the situation was not much different. A prime example, and a source of great political difficulty for the president, was Chicago. The problem here was *de facto* segregation, but it was segregation nonetheless. This led to a cutoff of funds in Chicago, where $34 million was withheld because of racial discrimination. An outraged Mayor Daley, Democratic kingmaker and a vocal representative of white ethnic voters in the city, lobbied President Johnson, who quickly caved in and ordered the funding restored. The Office of Education later claimed that the problem stemmed from housing patterns beyond the reach of Title VI. The problem was how to effect greater racial balance in the face of Title I of the 1964 Civil Rights Act, which prohibited such measures.

A full-blown controversy erupted the next year, 1966, when Alabama Governor George Wallace signed an order declaring

HEW's desegregation guidelines "null and void" and prohibiting their enforcement by state officials. An investigation of school integration by the Civil Rights Commission in 1966 blamed the South's use of "freedom of choice" plans for the lack of desegregation. By 1967 the Civil Rights Commission reported little progress toward further desegregation despite the threat of a federal funds cutoff. As with other Great Society issues, the question of race shaped much of the debate over educational opportunity in the United States.

Publication of the 1966 Coleman Report (*Equality of Educational Opportunity*) further inflamed the controversy. Commissioned under the 1964 Civil Rights Act, the report found that racial segregation predominated in the nation's public schools and that minority students had less access to laboratories, good libraries, college preparatory courses, and good textbooks than did their white counterparts. Not surprisingly, perhaps, minority students also had poorer teachers, lower standardized test scores, and lower high school graduation rates than white students. None of this was news. But, using regression analysis, the report argued that "school factors" were *not* responsible for most of that difference. Much more important were "family background and socioeconomic factors." Coleman's summary traced the complexity of the problem: "the sources of inequality of educational opportunity appear to be first in the home itself and the cultural influences immediately surrounding the home; then they lie in the schools' ineffectiveness to free achievement from the impact of the home, and in the schools' homogeneity which perpetuated the social influences of the home and its environments."

Even this was not completely new. During Senate hearings on ESEA, Roger Freeman of the Hoover Institution had testified to a correlation between "family income, low educational achievements, and unemployment." Although the Coleman

Report made no recommendations for change, it suggested that educational opportunity, much like economic opportunity, was more complicated than most liberals admitted. Certainly Lyndon Johnson's vision of the Great Society unleashing a wave of opportunity that would sweep before it the ills of the past was overly simplistic—in education as in economics. Conservatives opposed to integration hailed the Coleman Report but avoided grappling with the transformative structural changes in school and home environments that it suggested were necessary for lasting change. The public at large supported Title I funding as the avenue to educational opportunity.

Advocates for children, such as Marian Wright Edelman, later complained that "too much of the debate on ESEA . . . focused on the cognitive achievement of children, and too little on the equally crucial intended target of Title I: the institutional behavior of schools." In addition, publication of "A Bill of Rights for Children" from the Hunt Task Force on Child Development in 1966–1967 provided contradictory evidence. Chaired by Illinois psychologist Joseph Hunt, this task force urged earlier intervention and an expanded Head Start program. It also complained that funding remained woefully inadequate, noting that in 1967, 19 million persons over sixty-five (who voted) had received $25.7 billion in benefits while 24 million children (who did not vote) had received $2 billion. What remained uncertain was the extent to which additional monies could effect educational change.

Compounding the debate was the interaction of race with education—in personal lives, institutional structures, and policymaking. Publication of a 1967 government report on *Racial Isolation in the Public Schools* highlighted this issue. It suggested that money was not the answer to the country's educational ills and would not provide opportunity for the disadvantaged to escape poverty. Massive racial integration was much more important, the study concluded. But by 1967 race had replaced civil rights on the nation's agenda, and race was an issue that fostered divisiveness rather than forged consensus.

The other major difficulty with Title I of ESEA lay in its efforts to target the poor. As the historian Allen Matusow has argued, most local districts accepted the money but not the objectives it was meant to fulfill. They used the funds to keep local taxes down and extend benefits to the children of their middle-class voters rather than target the poor as intended by the legislation. Entrenched bureaucrats refused to change their habits and take risks. Whether or not the application of significant funds could improve the educational opportunities, and thus the educational achievements, of poor children was never really tested. For political and bureaucratic reasons, ESEA monies were diluted so that virtually everyone received a piece of the action. Low achievement replaced poverty as the benchmark for the use of these monies at the local level. By the early 1970s, when early evaluations first became available, publication of the Gardner study revealed that from 1965 to 1969 the percentage of federal aid to overall educational expenditures was too small to have significant impact. Wealthy suburbs, not impoverished urban or rural districts, continued to benefit most.

Less controversial was another key educational aid program. The Higher Education Act of 1965 found widespread bipartisan support and for the first time funded federal scholarships ("educational opportunity grants") for undergraduates. It also provided additional grants for the construction of classrooms, monies for libraries and instructional equipment, a National Teachers Corps, and funds to improve undergraduate courses. Republicans opposed federal student loan guarantees and complained about the speed with which the bill was considered, but generally they supported its major provisions.

In 1966 Congress authorized more funds under ESEA than the president requested, and expanded the program. Although the changes did not take effect until 1968 because of the shaky fiscal situation in 1967, they added to the program's costs. States could base Title I requests on the national average per pupil expenditure for education rather than the state's own average (if the former was higher), and Congress raised the family income level for eligibility from $2,000 to $3,000 (the figure used in the antipoverty program), thereby bringing an additional 300,000 children under the provisions of Title I.

Only two years later the political landscape had changed. In the 1966 elections Republicans gained forty-seven seats in the House and three in the Senate. When LBJ proposed amendments to ESEA in 1967, he met resistance. The president proposed to reauthorize the Teachers Corps and expand commitments and funding under the 1965 legislation. House Democrats wanted even more. In the words of New York's Hugh Carey, the administration was "talking like Midas but . . . funding like Oliver Twist."

But Republicans, led by Albert Quie of Minnesota, tried to substitute block grants to the states for the categorical grants in the refunding of ESEA. This was more than a dispute over the packaging of funds, for block grants would shift the responsibility to determine local needs from the federal government and the U.S. Office of Education to the states. Administration opposition stemmed not only from a reluctance to relinquish power but from a conviction that the states could not manage the programs and that urban areas would be denied their fair share of the monies. Labor, church groups, and civil rights organizations mobilized to back the administration and successfully overcame efforts by the U.S. Chamber of Commerce and state school officers in support of the Quie amendment. The block-grant proposal probably met defeat, however, because it raised the church-state issue again. Several state laws prohibited public aid to parochial schools, and the shift of funds would seemingly violate the child-benefit theory that had enabled the legislation to pass two years earlier.

Having dodged that bullet, the administration fell victim to another. Democratic Representative Edith Green of Oregon successfully shifted Title III funds (for innovative educational centers) to the block-grant approach with support from Southern Democrats and Republicans. The House also adopted an amendment prohibiting the government from withholding funds from local school districts who failed to comply with the Civil Rights Act until they had been found in noncompliance by the entire course of legal procedure. As in the past, the Senate eliminated the restriction in the final bill. It did so, however, only after receiving assurances from HEW Secretary John Gardner that adequate warnings would be given to local school districts, assurances that headed off a threatened Southern filibuster but guaranteed that enforcement would slow. Even more ominous was Senator Everett Dirksen's proposal to prohibit the use of federal funds for busing students or reassigning teachers to redress racial imbalance. After lengthy debates and several procedural votes, Dirksen eventually withdrew his amendment. The issue remained a sign of the persistent intrusion of race in educational issues. Final congressional action came only in the final hour before adjournment, and Congress extended the programs through fiscal 1971.

As passed, the Elementary and Secondary Education Amendments of 1967 contained one other provision that seemed insignificant at the time but came to have great educational and political importance—a provision for bilingual Spanish-English education, introduced by Senator Ralph Yarborough of Texas. None of the education task forces had raised the issue, chiefly because bilingual experiments seemed possible under existing legislation. But Yarborough needed Mexican-American support for reelection, and his proposal sought to solidify that support.

As the educational historian Diane Ravitch has noted, the bilingual proposal rested on several assumptions: that Hispanic children needed a stronger concept of self, that their negative self-image stemmed in part from the apparent "uselessness" of their native tongue, that instruction in their native language would remedy this, and that bilingual instruction would also instill pride in their cultural heritage. Whether or not these assumptions were true, linguistic minorities seized on them to demand that school districts provide instruction in their native languages as well. The real issue, however, lay in the intent of the program. Was it designed to provide a transition from a native tongue to English? Or was its purpose to maintain native languages and preserve existing differences? Observers on both sides of the issue usually extended their analysis from language to culture, which to critics raised the question of assimilation or pluralism. As the United States moved toward more of a multicultural society, this issue of immigrant traditions and national culture inflamed passions on both sides. Was the United States to be a melting pot or a salad bowl, and were the two mutually exclusive? In 1974 the Supreme Court ruled (in *Law v. Nichols*) that schools needed to create special language programs for non-English-speaking children, but the Court failed to resolve the controversy because it did not specify whether the programs should serve a maintenance or transitional purpose. By the 1970s the country had "discovered" ethnicity, so the issue was more inflammatory than ever.

Unlike health care, which enjoyed broad public support but attracted strong opposition from the medical community, federal aid to education enjoyed broad support from both the public and educators. This encouraged Congress to be more generous. In 1968, for instance, Congress overwhelmingly authorized almost twice as much for education as President Johnson requested, even though LBJ was a lame duck with little power. The House approved the 1968 Higher Education Amendments by a vote of 389 to 15. Between 1965 and 1968 the number of college students receiving federal aid more than doubled (to 1,175,000) and their funding more than tripled (to more than $1 billion).

Lyndon Johnson had wanted to be the "education president," and in many respects he succeeded. By the time he left office in 1969 he had steered at least sixty education laws through Congress. Passage in 1965 of the Elementary and Secondary Education Act, as well as the Higher Education Act, dramatically changed education in the United States. Central to that change was not only the availability of federal monies but a new philosophy that endorsed access and opportunity for all who qualified. No longer should poor but bright students be denied a chance at higher education. No longer should children in financially impoverished school districts be denied basic laboratory and library resources that their peers in richer districts enjoyed. The federal government would provide the funds to equalize access and opportunity. It didn't always work that way, of course, because political considerations mandated that almost everyone everywhere (particularly if they voted) share in the new largesse.

4

Model Cities

THE 1950s were the heyday of the suburb in American life, when Americans flocked to what the historian Kenneth Jackson called the "crabgrass frontier." But by the 1960s the city increasingly commanded the American consciousness. The difference in tone and substance between the two eras and locales was profound. Although suburban life ultimately found its share of critics, who lamented its homogeneity ("little boxes" as Malvina Reynolds sang) and its celebration of a consumption-oriented capitalism, many (especially the residents) viewed it as the fulfillment of the American Dream. Home ownership, a private yard, the backyard barbeque, a car (perhaps two) in the driveway—all symbolized "making it" for their owners, who were almost certainly white and middle class. But if "making it" meant living in the suburbs, cities attracted attention in the 1960s because of their environmental and demographic problems, because their political and social mechanisms seemed to be breaking down. The Model Cities program was a response to those problems and represented the premier legislative achievement of the Great Society's final two years.

Federal aid to urban areas was not new. During the 1950s and early 1960s a passion for urban renewal had swept the United States, though "renewal" proved to be something of a misnomer. It generally meant razing historic structures or bulldozing older sections of cities (often those populated by ethnic and racial minorities), followed by the construction of expressways, massive office buildings, or sterile housing projects. In many cities urban renewal came to mean "Negro removal," and for families in almost every case it meant forced relocation rather than renewal. One important result was a housing shortage. For every unit of low-income housing constructed during the 1950s, urban renewal destroyed four units. Demolition of commercial and manufacturing establishments usually accompanied this destruction of housing, often wiping out entire communities. By the mid-1960s many city planners believed that urban renewal had damaged more than it had revitalized the fabric of urban life, and they sought to salvage some of the wreckage.

The Economic Opportunity Act of 1964, with its Community Action Program, tried to give local populations the power to effect change, but it failed to focus specifically on the urban infrastructure and physical environment. As the *Washington Post* editorialized in May 1964:

> The President summoned the country to build cities to which future generations will come not just to live, but to live the good life. That we are so far failing to do this is made doubly deplorable by the fact that here and there our planners and architects and construction engineers demonstrate plainly that they have the creative capacity, the scientific skill, and the ingenuity to make urban life good. But the occasional exhibition of their art is concealed largely by the mediocre, the illy planned, the badly designed. Cities are being rebuilt at a very rapid rate, but much of the rebuilding is tasteless, cheerless, and unimaginative. The rate of new construction is so rapid that in a few decades we are

going to have a great many virtually new cities, but we cannot say with as much confidence that they will be better
cities.

The Housing Act of 1964 avoided larger urban issues by
simply extending existing programs for one year. Neither the
president nor the Congress was ready to move. The *New York
Times* warned that LBJ had to do more if he intended to realize his Great Society. Major changes were needed, the paper
argued, if "the big city is to remain a place for ordinary people
to live as well as work, and if the suburbs are to become more
than an ugly sprawl and a commuter's nightmare."

In 1965, to begin a process of change, Congress passed a
Housing and Urban Development Act. Under consideration
since the Kennedy administration and hailed as the most significant legislation of its type since the Housing Act of 1949,
the 1965 act proposed a broad plan of federal aid for the rest of
the decade. Perhaps its most important feature was an effort
to provide low-income housing different from traditional
public housing, in part through rent supplements to encourage private-sector development of housing for the poor. Rent
supplements—where an individual paid a fourth of his income for rent in private housing and the government contributed the rest—were extremely controversial. They could
be used in any neighborhood, which meant that black families
might move into predominantly white areas. Conservatives
claimed that rent supplements were "foreign to American
concepts" and would "disrupt the social patterns of the nation" by mingling low- and middle-income families, thereby
creating "socio-economic integration." Republicans charged
that they represented socialism, threatened home ownership,
and "would kill the initiative of the American family to im-

prove its living accommodations by its own efforts." Congress ultimately limited the subsidies to individuals who already qualified for public housing.

The 1965 legislation passed easily behind strong Democratic majorities, though opponents later marshaled sufficient votes to deny fiscal 1966 funding for rent supplements. As Illinois Senator Paul Douglas warned, if "we ignore the basic fact that cities were built for people to serve human needs—our entire Nation will soon falter and decline." Other supporters of the bill, such as Representative Henry B. Gonzalez of Texas, considered urban aid essential to the antipoverty effort, for "poverty cannot be fought unless we fight the slums, the dilapidated and substandard housing, and the urban blight which are the breeding grounds of poverty." The measure called for the construction of 200,000 new public housing units during the next four years, but by 1967 annual construction reached only 23,000.

In a lengthy analysis of urban renewal, inserted into the *Congressional Record* by the bill's supporters, urbanologist Herbert Gans proposed that the solution to transforming the cities lay not in more slum clearance but in a program of urban housing. With words that now sound prophetic, he argued that

> From a political point of view, it is urgently necessary to begin integrating the suburbs and to improve housing conditions in the city before the latter becomes an ominous ghetto of poor and increasingly angry Negroes and Puerto Ricans, and the suburbs become enclaves of affluent whites who commute fearfully to a downtown bastion of stores and offices.

Gans warned that any housing efforts would fail in the absence of more jobs. Much more than mere coordination was needed. As a first step toward urban revitalization, in September 1965 Congress approved legislation creating a Department of Housing and Urban Development (HUD).

That same year LBJ's Task Force on Urban Problems, chaired by political scientist Robert Wood of the Massachusetts Institute of Technology, advocated a "demonstration cities" program to address the problems of low- and moderate-cost housing, to link physical reconstruction with social programs, and to cut bureaucratic red tape through more flexible building regulations and trade practices. Social scientists believed that urban revitalization needed only rational planning to succeed, and they banked on the "fiscal dividend" generated by the 1964 tax cut and continued economic growth to fund their efforts. In many respects the vision was a naive one. As one study of urban problems later described the plan: the "stubborn facts of interest group politics, limited budgets, bureaucratic resistance to change, and the extreme pluralism of American society faded away before the image of a well-conceived federal blueprint for the slums, backed by a President with enormous power."

The Wood task force drew upon numerous resources, but two influences seem particularly strong. One was a two-page memorandum by Antonia Chayes, a former Wood student, and Leonard Duhl, a psychiatrist who headed the Office of Planning of the National Institute of Mental Health. They proposed a shift from "bricks and mortar" to a "social and psychological" program. United Auto Workers President Walter Reuther later seized this idea, commissioned a proposal for Detroit (which nonetheless still embraced the bulldozer mentality), and caught the ear of the president at the very moment Lyndon Johnson was preparing his 1966 legislative agenda.

The second influence was the experience of New Haven, Connecticut. During the 1950s New Haven had engaged in the sort of urban renewal that was now under attack, razing buildings and disrupting communities. But late in that decade the city changed to focus on the problems of people in the city, especially the poor. In 1962 it received a $2.5 million grant from the Ford Foundation to link human renewal with the physical rehabilitation of the city. Under the leadership of Mayor Richard Lee, New Haven pioneered in what two years later became a national economic opportunity program. Lee brought in Edward Logue, an urban developer who later moved on to Boston and New York, to reshape New Haven's urban landscape. But Mayor Lee's vision guided the city. In a December 1962 speech he lamented that "the haphazard growth of our cities and the years of neglect and lack of comprehensive planning have resulted not only in physical ugliness, chaos, and decay; they have also produced the terrible by-product of human waste and suffering." Bulldozers were not the answer; they were no substitute for human services. Private funds were obviously insufficient to tackle the country's urban problems. Something much more comprehensive was needed.

During the summer of 1965 President Johnson established a second task force to prepare legislative recommendations for a full-scale urban program. In December 1965 this task force issued its report, calling for the establishment of sixty-six experimental programs in cities across the country. The report recommended selecting cities of various sizes: six with a population of more than 500,000; ten with between 250,000 and 500,000 residents; and fifty with a population under 250,000. The program would focus on run-down sections of those cities; mobilize, concentrate, and coordinate resources to combat persistent problems; and run for five years. A month later, in late January 1966, President Johnson sent Congress a message on "City Demonstration Programs" that embraced these recommendations.

The president opened his remarks with a plea that "Nineteen-sixty-six can be the year of rebirth for American cities," and warned that without a new urban program the United States was in danger of becoming "two people—the suburban affluent and the urban poor." Johnson embraced the new model of urban change, noting the "social and psychological effects of relocating the poor." The purpose was to change "the total environment of the area affected." This meant not only housing conditions but "schools, parks, playgrounds, community centers, and access to all necessary community facilities." One of the proposal's chief architects, Charles Haar, captured the essence of the effort when he noted that it was conceived "synergistically."

Although LBJ labeled this a "demonstration cities" bill, he rejected task force recommendations that a limited number of cities be selected as experimental projects. Instead the president observed that there were "few cities or towns in America which could not participate in the Demonstration Cities Program." This was, of course, a political move to secure congressional support. But as the number of participating cities multiplied they diluted available funds, and the concept of a social-scientific "experiment" to see what worked and what did not never materialized. Other parts of the proposal included an emphasis on metropolitan regional planning, a renewed nondiscriminatory housing program, the construction of "new communities," rent supplements to provide more low-income housing, and additional funds for urban mass transportation. All of this was to be administered by the new Department of Housing and Urban Development. The effort would be expensive, Johnson admitted, but it did not compare "in cost with the ugliness, hostility, and hopelessness of unliv-able cities."

By 1966 dramatic events had focused public and congres-sional attention on the nation's cities. Foremost among them were the urban riots that depicted cities as cauldrons of racial prejudice, human squalor, exploitation, and joblessness. To-gether with a landscape of deteriorating or burned-out build-ings and rat-infested tenements, these conditions mirrored the failure of urban institutions, triggering white flight and a fear that urban decay threatened the social stability of the nation. The urban environment seemed a powder keg of social dyna-mite. As HUD Secretary Robert Weaver later admitted, "I am sure that Model Cities would never have come out of the Con-gress if it were not for the riots."

Although conservative arguments that urban riots were es-sentially criminal behavior would later find widespread ac-ceptance, in 1966 the prevailing view was that the riots stemmed from a legacy of economic, political, and racial prob-lems. As such they represented not only an effort to find jobs and share power but a cry for help. The Commission on Civil Disorders reported that "domestic turmoil had [apparently] become part of the American scene." The answer, in short, was not a punitive focus on law and order but new programs to ameliorate deplorable conditions and enhance opportunity. Model Cities proposed to coordinate an attack on urban blight and restructure the urban environment.

Despite this impetus, Congress hesitated to endorse the pro-gram. During debates on the bill in August, Senator Abraham Ribicoff of Connecticut held hearings on the "crisis in the cities" to dramatize the plight of urban areas and their resi-dents. Attorney General Nicholas Katzenbach testified that "agitators" had indeed fomented the riots, but that the Demonstration Cities approach was just the remedy. The agitators, he said, were "disease and despair, joblessness and hopelessness, rat-infested housing and long-impacted cynicism. These sources of agitation are not the product of Communists or Black Nationalists or terrorists. They are the product of a generation of indifference by all the American people to the rot and rust and mold which we have allowed to eat into the core of our cities." New York Senator Robert Kennedy called for a domestic Marshall Plan to attack urban problems, complaining that we "give our money and go back to our homes and maybe our swimming pools and wonder, why don't they keep quiet, why don't they go away?" But his congressional colleagues seemed more concerned about the growth of federal power and escalating racial violence. Shifts in the civil rights movement by 1966, together with an increasing OEO focus on racial minorities, exacerbated the problem by making urban relief appear to be another program chiefly for African Americans.

The Ribicoff hearings, however, mobilized support for an attack on urban problems. Urban mayors from both political parties demanded that something be done. New York City Mayor John Lindsay testified that two million of his city's residents lived in poverty, that more than a quarter of the housing stock was substandard, with over 350,000 dwelling units having been constructed before 1900, and that the city spent 14 percent of its budget on welfare (though half of the city's welfare expenditures went to slumlords because of the lack of public housing). New York City needed $50 billion during the next decade to address these problems. Nationwide more than seven million urban homes were run-down and at least three million still lacked adequate plumbing. Lindsay told another congressional committee that even $50 billion would be insufficient: "We have learned that these building programs do not of themselves attack the hard-core causes of poverty and blight. Over time, it has become painfully clear that much more than physical renewal is needed."

Detroit Mayor Jerome Cavanagh estimated the price tag for a full-scale commitment to urban change to be more than $500 billion. Detroit alone, he noted, needed $15 billion during the next decade. Local finances were completely inadequate even to begin the job, but he warned that care "must be exercised not to build up anticipations beyond our capabilities to achieve." In some cities, such as Los Angeles, the problem was as much structural as financial. Mayor Sam Yorty testified that while he controlled police, fire, sanitation, and recreation facilities, he had no control over the city's schools, transportation, employment, health, welfare, and housing. Coordination of urban services was needed before the city's problems could be addressed.

The Demonstration Cities and Metropolitan Development Act announced that "Congress hereby finds and declares that improving the quality of urban life is the most critical domestic problem facing the United States." The bill included ten sections. The key was Title I, which provided for comprehensive city demonstration programs to address the total urban environment and provide federal support for up to 80 percent of the cost of each program. It also outlined a list of criteria that each plan had to meet. The most important required that every proposal demonstrate its ability to make a "significant impact" on urban blight and its accompanying physical and social problems. The purpose, in short, was to reverse deterioration through community development, not merely to slow or ameliorate urban decay.

Title II reached beyond specific cities to embrace surrounding metropolitan areas. Metropolitan planning and coordination were essential because no area was isolated. New York Mayor John Lindsay's testimony highlighted this when he noted that 3.5 million commuters daily entered Manhattan south of Central Park. Title II also specifically prohibited the secretary of housing and urban development from requiring the busing of children or any other program to achieve racial balance in a metropolitan area as a condition for receiving a grant.

The remaining titles focused on an array of measures designed to facilitate urban development and improve access to housing. Title III broadened the home loan mortgage insurance program for veterans. Title IV authorized insurance for developers of new towns and communities and offered greater flexibility to developers. Title V authorized a new mortgage insurance program for group medical practices. Title VI provided for historic and architectural preservation in urban renewal programs and sought to stimulate new methods of historic preservation, while Title VII created greater flexibility in what localities could count toward their share of urban renewal costs and emphasized the need for more low- and moderate-cost housing. The final sections of the bill sought to improve access to housing for rural residents, created a new federal program to provide technical assistance to solve urban problems, and created a new program of grants and loans to provide housing for natives and other needy persons in Alaska.

Senate discussion on the bill was focused and relatively brief. Led by Maine's Edmund Muskie, chosen chiefly because he did *not* represent an urban area, the Senate defeated an amendment offered by conservative Republican John Tower of Texas to eliminate funding for demonstration cities and leave only planning funds. As Tower noted at the time, the vote on that amendment was essentially a vote on the bill itself. In mid-August the Senate passed the full bill by a vote of 53 to 22, with twenty-five senators not voting.

Debate in the House was bitter and concentrated on the issues of federal power and race. Republicans attacked the proposal for its dangerous shift of power to the White House and various federal agencies. Dave Martin of Nebraska warned that it "aims at nothing less than a remaking of our cities according to a Federal master plan." Although Texas Democrat Wright Patman defended the measure as an exercise in "creative federalism," House Republicans attempted to remove Title I and restrict federal expenditures to planning. Democrat William Barrett of Pennsylvania charged that the program was a "gimmick to centralize power." Joe Waggoner of Louisiana went even further, insisting that the cities were "practically beyond help." The legislation would increase federal power, he complained, but little else—because "the cities have long since exceeded their ability to provide the services needed for the people who live therein." Defenders of the legislation argued that the Model Cities program represented a new kind of federalism in that it encouraged cities to devise their own mechanisms for citizen involvement (a lesson learned from earlier community action debates) and provided block grants instead of categorical grants to fund local programs. The House Banking and Currency Committee reported: "This is to be a local program, planned and carried out by local people and based on local judgment as to the city's needs and its order of priorities in meeting these needs."

New York Republican Paul Fino was the point man for those who raised the issue of race. The legislation, he charged, was actually a civil rights bill in disguise. It would give Housing Secretary Robert Weaver and Education Commissioner Harold Howe "incredible power" to "control American metropolitan housing, educational, and living patterns." Fino linked that power to black militants. "Vote against this bill," he thundered in the House, "if you believe in localities having a right to draw up their own civil rights ordinances. Vote against this bill if you think that the time has come to draw the line and stand up to black power." He charged that the entire program was a "tool of black power" and warned that he could "imagine the kind of demonstration program black power has in mind. Demonstration conflagration. Demonstration incineration." Although Fino's diatribe attracted few adherents, he did pinpoint an underlying theme that even the bill's supporters admitted was there—the need to find some way to attack *de facto* segregation in Northern cities.

The measure, countered Henry B. Gonzalez of Texas, was the "real antiriot bill of the 89th Congress." Despite the bill's multiplicity of local programs, Fino insisted that federal guidelines would prevail precisely because the federal government held the purse strings. The "whole concept," he warned, "is to use Federal bribes in sewer, highway, transportation, and similar programs as part of a package to force cities to plan housing and schools the Weaver-Howe way." That threatened, in his view, to "undermine the American social and political fabric of local government and neighborhood schools." But Fino's amendments were defeated, and the House passed the measure 178 to 141, with 111 representatives not voting. While the large number recorded as not voting largely reflected the bill's timing, coming as it did just before adjournment in an election year, it left open the dangerous possibility that no majority really favored the measure.

After a quick reconciliation between the different versions of the bill, both houses passed the measure in mid-October, diluting many of the program's innovative features. Congress declared that the legislation was not intended to change the allocation of funds among cities, and authorized additional funding for traditional urban renewal. It also frustrated the effort to appoint federal coordinators to help cities obtain necessary resources, and asked HUD to move ahead with projects designed at the local level.

President Johnson signed the legislation on November 3, 1966, though it provided much less long-term funding than he had requested. At the same time he changed its name from the Demonstration Cities program to the Model Cities program, largely because he feared its association with the word "demonstration" after a summer of urban riots.

Under the new legislation, cities began with planning grants. Once these were approved, the cities then applied for a range of federal grants and HUD "supplemental grants" to implement their plans. The first planning phase ended in early 1969, and a second group of cities received planning grants in late 1968 so they could begin implementation in 1970. Each program was to create a City Demonstration Agency (CDA) whose leadership was appointed by and responsible to the mayor. The act also required Model Cities neighborhood residents to play a significant role in developing and carrying out the program. An elected citizens board advised the CDA, and successful projects were to employ local residents. Section 103(a) of the act required CDAs to provide "maximum opportunities for employing residents of the area in all phases of the program and enlarged opportunities for work and training." Despite this requirement, by 1969 less than half of all salaried employees in seventy-seven projects were residents of the target neighborhoods.

Like the economic opportunity and Medicare programs before it, Model Cities discovered new problems faster than it could generate solutions for them. It was also underfunded. Despite the selection of 150 "model cities," from 1968 to 1972 only 18 percent of HUD's community development aid budget went to poverty neighborhoods. As Charles Haar later noted, Model Cities "was a complex conception, vague in its outlines, which was supposed to be fleshed out through experimentation and experience." But Congress was becoming increasingly uneasy with it.

The changed political climate was also evident in congressional treatment of Johnson's 1966 fair housing proposal. Although housing programs represented a key part of the Great Society's efforts at urban revitalization, opponents characterized fair housing as a threat to the nation and, led by Republican Senator Everett Dirksen, focused their attention more on antibusing measures and other anti–civil rights measures, including a law banning "outside agitators" from crossing state lines to "incite" a riot. A conservative filibuster ultimately prevented consideration of the fair housing bill, but liberals had long considered passage of effective legislation hopeless.

Twenty states did enact fair housing legislation in 1966, but a backlash emphasizing the rights of property owners developed, and several cities passed "homeowners' rights" ordinances. Martin Luther King's efforts to bring the civil rights movement north to Chicago failed in the face of angry white mobs. The fair housing issue eventually brought down California Governor Edmund "Pat" Brown and elected Ronald Reagan as his successor. National surveys in 1967 and 1968 reflected contradictory public attitudes on housing. Almost 70 percent agreed that blacks should have equal housing opportunities, but 63 percent of whites opposed any law prohibiting housing discrimination. When Congress appropriated funds for housing that year, it granted substantially less than what the administration requested. The civil rights coalition had lost not only its moral presence but its political clout.

Another continuing obstacle to change was the attitude of local officials. All too often they saw Model Cities as an opportunity to secure funds rather than as a chance to restructure their urban environment through social engineering. Indeed, since Model Cities funds were administered through local agencies, the prospects for significant change were slim. That was why those same officials worried so much about the Community Action Programs, for these actually held the promise of change. But with the war against the CAPs ongoing, and with the administration under increasing attack in Washington, local officials rarely felt any real pressure to effect change. When Newark, New Jersey, received Model Cities funds in 1967, for example, its city council decided to bulldoze 150 acres of ghetto housing to construct a medical and dental college rather than improve low- and moderate-income housing. This scarcely helped to alleviate the national housing shortage, then estimated at 26 million units for the next decade. The problem with Model Cities, in short, was not too much federal supervision but too little.

Model Cities, or any other urban resuscitation program, also faced an economic dilemma. Not only would a full-scale attack on urban problems probably exceed the capability of the American tax system to provide sufficient revenues—regardless of a war in Vietnam or an inflationary economy—but the urban economic base for continued progress was simply not there. The problem was jobs. Since 1948, population and jobs had fled steadily from the central cities to the suburbs. Manufacturing, wholesale and retail trade, and a growing service economy moved to the suburbs in search of cheap land, new buildings, and tax breaks. They not only took with them their jobs but their contributions to the urban tax base. Three years before Congress enacted Model Cities, more than half of all manufacturing employment was in the suburbs, and this trend continued to accelerate. Although in the short term an expansion of public (especially government) employment masked the implications of this shift, public jobs simply imposed additional burdens on taxing authorities and further reduced the funds available for rehabilitation projects.

The urban environment, constantly changing, presented planners with new challenges even before Model Cities programs took effect. Events in 1967 indicated a sharp escalation of tensions and galvanized the president and Congress to discuss additional programs even before Model Cities had moved beyond the planning stages. (Not until December 1968 did HUD announce approval of the first Comprehensive Development Plan, for Seattle.) The central concern in 1967 was the outbreak of urban rioting and the reluctant response of Congress to its causes.

July 23, 1967, brought the most destructive urban riot of the sixties, in Detroit. Early the next morning, Michigan Governor George Romney asked the White House for federal assistance, and Lyndon Johnson put federal troops on alert. While the governor and the president danced a political two-step, each looking ahead to the 1968 elections and seeking to preserve or enhance his own reputation, conditions in the city ran to waste. Federal troops arrived to find fires burning unattended and widespread looting.

The Detroit riot symbolized both the problems and frustrations of urban policy in the 1960s. As historian Sidney Fine noted in his study of the riot, Detroit appeared to be a model city, and the riot surprised most observers. The automobile industry had prospered during the decade, and the black middle class had expanded. But beneath the public relations successes of Mayor Cavanagh's administration, problems festered. Housing stock in black neighborhoods compared poorly with that in white neighborhoods. More than 70 percent of the black population lived in the poorest areas of the city, and more than 60 percent were renters. Comparable figures for the white population were 17 percent and 35 percent.

Although the rise and success of black enterprises such as Motown Records had fostered an image of Detroit as a success story for African Americans, these anecdotes masked the larger reality. Detroit was a city whose racial divisions had rigidified since the end of World War II. Whites had formed almost two hundred neighborhood associations by 1965, designed essentially to preserve their neighborhoods from racial integration. Recent studies by Thomas Sugrue indicate that the escalation of racial hostility in Detroit predated both the civil rights movement and Great Society legislation. Later federal programs clearly exacerbated racial cleavages because they targeted particular constituencies and sought to equalize opportunity, but they did not initiate the politics of race.

Black discontent focused on a series of complaints: geographic segregation, lack of recreational facilities, problems with merchants, inadequate education, poor housing, police behavior, and a lack of jobs. Correction or amelioration of most of these problems was the goal of numerous Great Society programs already enacted. Only New York and Chicago, for example, had received more antipoverty funding than Detroit since passage of the 1964 Economic Opportunity Act. But the programs were either insufficient or irrelevant to the eradication of problems in Detroit. Human relations proved more of a trigger to the riot than economic issues.

As was the case with so many riots in the sixties, this one began with a police raid which coalesced black grievances and anger. Like the rioters, the police (and later the National Guard) lost their composure and engaged in physical violence. "They are savages," said one policeman about the rioters. "Those black son-of-a-bitches. I'm going to get me a couple of them before this is over." The riot shocked many liberals, who believed that Great Society legislation would solve such problems. In reality, the programs passed by Congress had only begun to operate. The stronger impact of the Detroit riot was on moderates and conservatives, who believed that the liberal programs of the Great Society were more than sufficient and failed to recognize either that they lacked adequate funding or that their implementation still lay largely in the future. As a result, both groups increasingly turned against federal programs and attacked liberal solutions.

Eventually army paratroopers put down the riot, along with seventeen thousand troops from the National Guard, the state police, and the Detroit police department. More than seven thousand persons were arrested (chiefly for looting), almost twice that of the 1965 Watts riot. Most of them were black males under age twenty-five. More than six hundred fire alarms sounded on July 24 alone, and Fine reported damage to "611 supermarkets, food and grocery stores; 537 cleaners and laundries; 326 clothing, department, and fur stores; 285 liquor stores, bars, and lounges; 240 drugstores; and 198 furniture stores." Convinced that a conspiracy lay at the heart of this riot and a similar one in Newark, President Johnson established a commission to report on causes and propose solutions. The Kerner Commission would report back the following year. But when the summer of 1967 came to a close, after more than 160 riots, President Johnson's approval rating on civil rights and racial turmoil had fallen to 32 percent.

Despite the well-documented problems of urban America, riots or no riots, Congress refused to commit itself to any further programs for the cities. A week after the Newark riot Congress joked about a $40 million rat-control bill, calling it a "civil rats" bill and dismissing it as a waste of money. Florida Democrat James Haley suggested that Congress instead invest in "a lot of cats and turn them loose." The bill failed, though

Congress received such criticism for its cavalier attitude that it later relented and included provisions for rat extermination in a Partnership for Health Act later that year.

Long and divisive debates characterized efforts to provide continuing funding for Model Cities and rent supplements. Congress funded Model Cities at less than half what the president wanted, and agreed to that only by a handful of votes; the House almost succeeded in restricting Model Cities funds to planning. That most planning grants went to cities represented by Democrats only solidified Republican hostility, though the reality was that most cities were Democratic political bastions. Congress also trimmed funding requests for housing programs. LBJ sought $40 million for rent supplements, but Congress granted only $10 million.

Critics complained that urban rehabilitation could be effective only with much larger funding commitments. In other words, once begun these programs would become expensive commitments. Even though urban areas admittedly needed revitalization, Republicans and Southern Democrats preferred to kill the entire program rather than provide adequate funding. Indeed, Congress now seemed more interested in punishing rioters than in addressing the conditions that spawned riots. Debates produced more rhetoric than legislation. Measures to make flag-burning or crossing state lines to incite a riot a federal crime passed the House but failed to make it through the Senate. HUD and the administration could sense the shifting mood. In the words of one HUD secretary: "We did not want the violence to undo the social reforms that had taken place in the mid-1960s. In fact, we were very careful *not* to allow a riot city to receive a lot of new money, as we didn't want to appear to respond to violence." Nonetheless studies reveal that of the 118 cities with one or more serious riots from 1964 to 1968, 83 applied for Model Cities funding and 69 received grants.

Symbolic of the shifting attitudes toward urban affairs was the administration's Safe Streets and Crime Control Act. In February 1967, in the face of rising crime rates, President Johnson issued a special message on crime. Originally designed to help states and communities improve and modernize their law enforcement, and based on a pilot study the preceding year, the bill emerged from Congress as something much more punitive. Congress insisted on block grants to the states (and not to communities) aimed chiefly at riots and organized crime. Although the House ultimately passed its own rewritten version of the measure, the Senate failed to pass any crime legislation. Congress clearly saw urban areas as a source of problems rather than opportunities.

By 1968 the urban crisis was without question the central social issue in the United States. In March, release of the Kerner Commission report emphasized both the dangers posed by urban problems and the price tag to rectify them. The report's failure to salute his administration for making progress upset President Johnson, so that he buried its findings. But the commission did praise the OEO programs for pointing the country in the right direction. It simply demanded that more be done.

The Kerner Commission singled out "white racism" as the chief cause of the urban crisis and warned that the nation was "moving toward two societies, one black, one white—separate and unequal." It found, despite President Johnson's insistence to the contrary, no conspiracy behind the riots. Oklahoma Senator Fred Harris, a commission member, later reported that they "encountered young black men, idling on the streets, who implored us to help them find work, and other blacks who were so angry that they could not bear to shake hands with us or look us in the face. We saw, close up, the human cost of wretched poverty and harsh racism." Life in the ghetto was one of "segregation and poverty," which had created a "destructive environment totally unknown to most white Americans." To those who argued that blacks and Hispanics could lift themselves up by their own bootstraps, just as had countless immigrants before them, the commission replied that there was now little demand for unskilled labor—in the ghetto or anywhere else.

The Kerner Commission's final report endorsed several basic principles for change. Programs needed to equal the dimensions of the problems and not be merely token responses, in order to make an immediate impact to "close the gap between promise and performance." New experiments were needed to "change the system of failure and frustration" that pervaded the ghetto, to counteract the racial isolation that threatened to create permanent social divisions. Even in its vague outlines this suggested a broad and costly program of social and economic reform, a program that LBJ believed too expensive to pass Congress, especially after the riots and with the rapidly escalating costs of the war in Vietnam. The commission argued that economic growth would fund new efforts but failed to consider the state of the economy, the limited funds that such growth would provide, and the war's drain on the treasury. The Kerner Commission's recommendations also went against the grain of public opinion, which by 1968 was increasingly disenchanted with liberal programs. Although this shift in public opinion seems to have occurred more from frustration than ideology, it boded ill for new programs.

A further difficulty with the Model Cities program became evident in the debate over the so-called Philadelphia Plan. Although Philadelphia billed itself as the City of Brotherly Love, it was little different from other urban areas in that race relations simmered just below the boiling point. To address issues of jobs and fairness, the Philadelphia Plan called for all city contract bids to specify the number of minority workers that would be hired. The building trades had long been a bastion of racial exclusion, and contractors opposed this effort at affirmative action. But the 1966 Model Cities law required urban rehabilitation programs to hire local minorities, though it set no quotas. By the fall of 1968 the General Accounting Office had declared the Philadelphia Plan illegal because it violated regulations requiring bidders to be informed of all job requirements in advance. In other words, although it avoided setting absolute quotas, which would have violated the 1964 Civil Rights Act, the plan was illegal because the city failed to establish the specific number of minorities to be hired.

Despite his failures in 1966 and 1967, President Johnson in 1968 once again proposed open housing legislation. Surprisingly, this time Congress enacted an open housing law, the first legislation of its kind in the twentieth century, to become fully effective in 1970. It proposed to prohibit discrimination in the sale or rental of housing, contained protections for civil rights workers and several antiriot provisions, and guaranteed the constitutional rights of American Indians. Congress, however, later denied all funding to enforce the open housing provisions of the 1968 civil rights bill.

The president also asked Congress for massive housing and urban development legislation in 1968. The 1968 housing bill was a dramatic change of course for the Congress, and was enacted with limited debate. It called for the construction of 26 million new homes and apartments over the next ten years. Six million of them would replace occupied substandard housing. The "rat" issue of 1967, when Congress had mocked the seriousness of urban problems by failing to enact a rat extermination measure, facilitated its passage. Republicans could ill afford a repeat performance, especially with the 1968 presidential election approaching. The other factor that attracted support was the omnibus nature of the bill. Few special-interest groups opposed it, chiefly because it contained something for almost everyone.

Written largely by the banking lobby, the Housing and Urban Development Act of 1968 contained various measures to expand home ownership. This had long been a Republican goal, and after some revisions the administration endorsed federal subsidies to enable low-income families to purchase their own homes (Section 235). Proponents believed this would transform riotous slum dwellers into responsible home owners. In the words of Democrat Henry Reuss of Wisconsin: "We think a man who owns his home is not likely to burn it down." Below-market interest programs had been part of the Housing Acts of 1961 and 1965, and they enabled for-profit private organizations to develop subsidized housing. But Section 235 essentially underwrote risks to developers rather than made housing more accessible to citizens. This section produced bipartisan support for the legislation despite the bill's expansion of rent supplements and Model Cities programs.

Although the inclusion of Section 235 enabled the 1968 Housing Act to pass Congress, the chief source of public concern remained the economic and racial integration of residential patterns. As Jill Quadagno noted in her study *The Color of Welfare,* "Housing as a welfare state issue cannot be divorced from housing as a racial issue." Two-thirds of the nation's poor were white, but federal programs increasingly targeted the urban poor, who were overwhelmingly nonwhite. Race loomed ever larger as a factor in public policy.

Even more important to the immediate formulation of policy was the influence of economics. The banking and real estate lobbies backed the 1968 bill precisely because it promised to feather their own nests, not because it represented sound public policy. As Quadagno observed, the banking lobby opposed "direct government subsidies to the poor, because new money pouring into the housing market would increase the money supply and lower interest rates." Instead it backed "an interest subsidy program, which would drive interest rates up." The bill also contained a rental program, Section 236, for families whose incomes exceeded public housing levels. Like the Section 235 provisions, the rental program also relied largely on private, for-profit developers and private mortgage financing. Since the government paid subsidies directly to the mortgage lender and not to the poor themselves, it was a banker's delight. It was also an outgrowth of the President's Committee on Urban Housing, established in 1967 and chaired by businessman Edgar Kaiser, which LBJ had instructed to "find a way to harness the productive power of America—which has proved it can master space and create unmatched abundance in the market place" through the creation of an effective federal housing program.

The final bill approved a three-year housing program to construct or rehabilitate more than 1.7 million housing units at a cost of $5.3 billion. It also authorized federal assistance to developers of new towns or communities, and provided a federal program of riot insurance. The measure easily passed the House, 226 to 135, and received approval in the Senate by voice vote. It became law with President Johnson's signature on August 1, 1968. Representative Byron G. Rogers, a Democrat from Colorado, exulted that "At one time the moon was out of reach. This is no longer true. Now, with this bill, a decent home will be within the reach of every American family." As had so often been the case, however, promise outran reality. All these federal programs together failed to equal the impact of the government's traditional middle-class housing policy financed by government-insured loans and income tax deductions.

The Republican Coordinating Committee, in an election-year attack on the Great Society, blamed the urban crisis on "the stewardship of the Democratic Administration." Despite its contradictions, the committee's report illustrated how much Republicans in the sixties shared the Democrats' concern with the urban crisis. On the one hand it affirmed Republican support for remedial urban legislation and, indeed, urged that more be done. "A fundamental problem of urban government," it declared, "is the inadequacy of available revenue sources." At the same time it attacked the Johnson administration for its ambitious efforts and excessive centralization of services, finding "little doubt" that the "repetition of irresponsible promises and political slogans by the Administration in 1964 and 1965 contributed to the violence and disorder of the succeeding two summers." The War on Poverty and the Great Society as a whole had been oversold, and extravagant promises that they would cure all ills had not only raised expectations but had led to a "sense of betrayal." The Republicans promised to do more—more money for job training, for education, and for housing, along with "fuller involvement of the poor in the solution of their own problems." In short, Republicans promised to do the same job but do it better and with a greater emphasis on the private sector and local authorities. This was a far cry from Republican estimates of the Great Society two decades later.

Given that Republicans not only promised to continue but expand the urban programs of the Great Society (a promise that the Nixon administration largely kept), what conclusions can we draw about Lyndon Johnson's urban programs? Because they emerged only in the final years of the Great Society, and were not scheduled to become effective until 1970, their stewardship fell to Johnson's Republican successor. Under Richard Nixon, Section 235 reactivated a slow housing market, accounting for 6 percent of all housing starts by 1971, before falling victim to the economic destabilization of the 1970s. Wartime inflation, White House neglect of the domestic economy, and a host of other factors led to "stagflation" that eventually left the program underfunded.

The Housing Act of 1968 sought to produce reform without structural change. Through federal subsidies and guarantees it hoped to "bribe" the private sector into making affordable housing more available, instead of financing decent housing for all citizens. Much of this low-income housing was shoddily constructed by private speculators.

The continued class and racial segregation of the nation's cities remained largely unresolved. Urban revitalization in the 1970s and after too often meant gentrification, which proved to be not all that dissimilar from the bulldozer mentality of the 1950s. It "revitalized" urban areas by focusing on the upscale refurbishing of older sections, which escalated home prices and pushed out the lower class and minorities. This led to further overcrowding and the deterioration of existing housing stock elsewhere in the city, and tightened class and racial residential boundaries. Sociologists such as Edward Banfield argued that the lower class produced slums as a matter of course, which all the new housing in the world would not remedy. The problem, according to Banfield, was one of attitude and culture. Although Banfield produced little evidence to support his argument, a variation on the culture-of-poverty theme, his cultural assertions and attack on the role of government found an audience and ultimately influenced urban policy.

The Great Society sought to develop a coordinated vision for urban and metropolitan planning. But the magnitude and intransigence of these problems, the unwillingness of suburban authorities to take responsibility for urban woes, and the lack of sufficient resources overwhelmed policymakers.

The interrelationship of so many urban issues led President Johnson to appoint a task force on government programs in 1967, but its suggestion that a program coordination office be established in the White House was not politically feasible by 1968 and failed to address the issue of resources. As HUD Secretary Robert Weaver complained in December 1968, participating agencies refused to relinquish control over their funds to any central coordinating body. As a result, he warned, "many model cities programs may be seriously underfunded," and the critical question of coordinating federal programs through state and local officials remained unresolved. The Nixon administration later tried its hand at finding solutions, with more block grants and expanded revenue sharing, but too often this only served to shift responsibility, not provide sufficient resources. In the 1980s the Reagan administration transferred virtually all responsibility to the states and cities but eliminated almost all federal resources. This led to the end of most programs and drove up local tax rates.

In a retrospective assessment, Robert Wood, who chaired the task force that proposed Model Cities, pointed to four prevailing criticisms of the program. Presidential and congressional "tampering" had politicized Model Cities; the program was "fiscally starved" from the outset; its regulations were too

complex and coordination procedures "unrealistic"; and as a
whole it was "too theoretical" to work in real life.

In addition, because of its timing the Model Cities program
became in effect an adjunct of the civil rights movement at the
very moment the movement shifted from an emphasis on
racial unity to one of Black Power, racial exclusion, and empowerment. This often led the public to see Model Cities as a
program only for minorities. At the outset this was not a liability, for there seemed to be a broad, biracial, middle-class
commitment to access and opportunity for all. But as issues of
civil rights became debates about race, the political atmosphere changed. As resources constricted, the public's willingness to expend tax monies to create additional resources
disappeared. When that happened, together with growing social divisions in the country and rising inflation, the middle
class withdrew its earlier commitment to solving the problems
of minorities, the poor, and the cities. This left Model Cities, in
the words of Charles Haar, "dead before reaching maturity."

The other major weakness of the Great Society's urban policy lay in its contradictory programs. As James Q. Wilson has
noted, the underlying problem was not any specific piece of
legislation but all of them together. What, specifically, did
LBJ's urban policy seek to accomplish? Rooted in Johnson's
consensus ideology as well as in the nature of American politics, Great Society policies simultaneously embraced several
contradictory programs. If suburban flight remained a source
of urban woes, why did FHA mortgage programs continue to
subsidize that flight? And why, given that reality, did urban
renewal programs try to counter it with their own subsidies?
Each goal seemed to be offset by another.

On a more positive note, studies of Model Cities experiments revealed the program to be the "single most effective

instrument to give the broadest range of services to disadvantaged areas and to improve local government operations," despite underfunding, bureaucratic red tape, and uneven levels
of citizen participation. In their study of federal urban aid,
Bernard Frieden and Marshall Kaplan reported that cities receiving grants under the program did concentrate these funds
in poverty neighborhoods for rehabilitation rather than destruction. Among peoples of all races and income levels,
Model Cities stimulated greater involvement in local affairs,
not only because it mandated community action but because it
gave local governments funds to disburse. A San Francisco re-
cipient noted that it "created organizations. It created aspir-
ants for higher office. . . . Model Cities was worth every
cent." Through its community programs and advisory groups
it provided a base for African-American and Hispanic efforts
to achieve political power. Between 1970 and 1980 the number
of black elected officials rose from 1,472 to 4,890.

What made progress difficult, with Model Cities as with
several other Great Society programs, was its focus on the
most debilitating conditions of urban life. Despite glib assurances that a prosperous economy would conquer those problems, there was no evidence to sustain that vision. In addition,
Model Cities was to be experimental in nature. It was to select
a very few cities, try out some programs to see if they worked
and had general application, and then perhaps develop a
broad national program. Politics emasculated that concept. It
became just one more in a blizzard of urban programs, 136 between 1963 and 1967 alone. Not only did the program include
more than twice the number of cities first envisioned, but neither Congress nor the public ever really viewed it as experimental. They demanded results, and when the results were
disappointing or slow to emerge, they attacked the program
with an eye to terminating it.

Ironically, as Robert Wood noted, not until after criticism of Great Society urban policies had become part of American political folklore did "reliable quantitative data concerning program results begin to appear." Analyses by Sar Levitan, Robert Taggart, Clifford Johnson, and Paul Ylvisaker "showed positive and statistically significant accomplishments." Others involved in the program, such as Charles Weltner, came to just the opposite conclusion. "We really believed that the combination of strategies that were decided upon would make a difference," he wrote in 1977 as Model Cities was winding down. "It is inescapable that we made very little difference and in some cases at least we clearly had a negative impact on the lives of the people we were sincerely trying to help."

The more people knew, the more complex the problems seemed, and the difficulties and costs of surmounting them multiplied. Consensus about the "best" solutions dissolved in the face of policy options. But by then the programs were caught in a backlash against civil rights and a growing opposition to federal intervention at state and local levels. By the time Model Cities was to have become fully operational, change had ceased to be a positive value for most Americans. Both major parties became steadily more conservative. At least in the political arena, the hopeful promise of the sixties as an era of possibilities collapsed.

In 1992 Attorney General William P. Barr told David Brinkley, "What we are seeing in the inner city [is] essentially the grim harvest of the Great Society." But blaming Model Cities, or any other Great Society program, for today's urban problems is more an exercise in political demagoguery than rational analysis. As William Julius Wilson has pointed out, continuing urban change has led to the social isolation of the urban poor. This demands more, not less, in the way of urban policy. The problem, Wilson argues, is lack of jobs. And Lyndon Johnson's urban programs sought to ameliorate conditions rather than change the social structure by creating jobs.

In the twenty years after 1967 Chicago lost 320,000 jobs in manufacturing; New York lost more than 500,000. The urban abandonment, not only white flight but middle-class flight, that policymakers noted in the sixties has accelerated since. Urban poverty rates, not surprisingly, have escalated dramatically, approaching what Wilson calls a "threshold of misery." Urban unemployment rates have doubled, though government statistics generally understate those rates. Family structure has deteriorated. In 1964 approximately three-fourths of African-American children under age six lived with two parents; by 1990 this figure had dropped to 37 percent. What emerged in these twenty years was a synergistic whirlwind of joblessness, crime, welfare dependency, and out-of-wedlock births. Urban life in the United States became more hazardous. The contribution of the 1960s was to move America's cities to the center of the country's political consciousness. The urban programs of the Great Society failed not so much because they were misguided but because they were woefully insufficient and because the nation's voters declined to make the sacrifices needed to make them work. The whirlwind of change that enveloped the country by the end of the sixties overwhelmed not only its resources but its consciousness.

5

Quality of Life

LYNDON JOHNSON'S vision of a Great Society embraced an array of legislative initiatives to improve Americans' "quality of life." Going beyond questions of access and opportunity, these measures assumed that the United States had moved into a society that left scarcity behind. The War on Poverty and other Great Society programs, along with economic growth, would resolve the "quantity" issue for individuals who still failed to share in the nation's material abundance. Soon they too would embrace the postscarcity, postindustrial ethos that marked the last third of the twentieth century. The issues that reflected this "quality" theme ranged from beautification to consumer rights to crime control. Some originated with the president (or, in the case of beautification, with his wife Lady Bird), others stemmed from the efforts of individual crusaders. In either case, this emphasis on improving the quality of life represented something new in the American experience.

Lyndon Johnson believed that many problems were "more of the spirit than of the flesh." Because of that, Great Society architect Richard Goodwin wrote, LBJ sought to "ensure our people the environment, the capacities, and the social structures which will give them a meaningful chance to pursue their individual happiness." Conservative critic William F.

Buckley, Jr., complained that this approach threatened to re-place individual decision-making with bureaucratic regula-tion. Human beings, he argued, traditionally "gave tone to that life, and they were its priests and poets." Buckley's com-plaints aside, not only were Lyndon Johnson's efforts to im-prove the quality of life for all Americans impressive, they had an enduring popularity even when other parts of the Great Society met withering criticism.

Since there was no overarching piece of legislation that de-fined quality-of-life issues, as there had been with civil rights, poverty, education, health care, or urban development, this part of the Great Society lacks easy definition or focus. The number of bills intended to improve the quality of Americans' lives was staggering, numbering in the hundreds. Consumer affairs, beautification, environmental protection, cultural life, and crime control were the dominant topics.

Consumer issues probably represented the most important of these efforts. In 1964 the president appointed Assistant Sec-retary of Labor Esther Peterson to be the first presidential as-sistant for consumer affairs. Her aggressive consumerism was something new for business, and they did not take to it kindly. The Advertising Federation of America labeled her "the most dangerous thing since Ghengis Khan." In 1967, wishing to court business more energetically in order to halt his declining popularity, the president replaced her with Betty Furness, a former television personality. But if he thought Furness would be a probusiness cipher, she proved him mistaken. She too be-came a strong voice for consumers.

The most significant advocate for consumers, however, came from outside the administration. He was Ralph Nader, who took on the automobile industry in a famous 1965 book, *Unsafe at Any Speed.* The auto industry was a bulwark of the American economy; indeed, the country's economic health was often measured by car sales. The industry was also home to the United Auto Workers, a powerful labor union whose staunch support of liberal causes provided the Democratic party with a phalanx of political workers and financial support. Nader was an independent sort with unquestioned integrity and a passionate social consciousness who quickly developed a reputation as a crusader for truth and justice. His personal life was spartan and his pursuit of corporate wrongdoers dogged. While an undergraduate at Princeton he had protested the use of DDT insecticide because it killed birds, and had worn a bathrobe to classes to object to student conformity in dress. As a muckraking attorney, he was unafraid to take on corporate giants as well as to suggest solutions to the problems they caused.

After graduation from Harvard Law School, Nader began his career working for Daniel Patrick Moynihan researching automobile safety in the Labor Department. Publication of *Unsafe at Any Speed* vaulted him into the public consciousness and launched his lifetime career as an analyst of corporate behavior. General Motors chairman James Roche later charged that Nader was starting a "crusade against corporations." Following publication of Nader's book on automobile safety defects (especially General Motors' Corvair), GM hired a private detective to "get something, somewhere on this guy to get him out of our hair and shut him up." This led to threatening telephone calls, efforts to entrap Nader in sexual affairs, and other invasions of his privacy as a citizen. Sales of his book skyrocketed along with public interest in auto safety. In 1966 the Junior Chamber of Commerce named Ralph Nader one of the nation's outstanding young men.

Nader's timing was impeccable. The highway death toll had risen steadily since 1960. Nader's book, subtitled "The Designed-in-Dangers of the American Automobile," blamed car design and construction for more human injuries and fatalities than were caused by accidents. Accidents would happen, but injuries could be prevented. Frederick Donner, GM's board chairman, admitted that the company spent only $1.25 million annually on safety out of profits of $1.7 billion. When auto industry executives tried to convince Congress that relaxation of the antitrust laws was the solution to automobile deficiencies, they met with disbelief and anger. Seeing broad public support for regulation, and given that it would have no significant budgetary impact, Lyndon Johnson became a consumer advocate. His 1966 State of the Union Message endorsed the National Traffic and Motor Vehicle Safety Bill.

This first legislation to regulate the automobile industry also marked the first major political defeat for that industry. The bill authorized the secretary of transportation to establish safety standards for automobiles. This led to requirements for head rests (to reduce whiplash injuries), padded dashboards, impact-absorbing steering wheels, more outside lights and reflectors to improve visibility, and seat belts for each passenger the car was designed to carry. Manufacturers who produced unsafe cars in violation of these standards faced civil penalties. In addition, if automobile companies discovered defects in their cars they were obligated to issue recall notices, informing car owners they had a defective product. Perhaps even more important than these provisions was the social consciousness raised by the measure. Consumers not only came to believe they had a right to safe products but to the swift correction of defects.

The atmosphere of the late sixties, with its suspicion of establishment institutions, was conducive to a Ralph Nader. But his was more than a fleeting popularity. After attacking automobile safety, Nader investigated a wide range of consumer issues. He also established the Center for the Study of Responsive Law and formed "Nader's Raiders," chiefly law students who established public interest research groups and developed a new generation of consumer activists. Under the scrutiny of Nader and his followers, corporate social conduct became a focus for federal legislation. Critics of the corporations, such as John Kenneth Galbraith in his *The New Industrial State* (1967), now charged that the tradition of business-government cooperation was a betrayal of liberalism. "Consumerism" became part of the new liberal agenda. Nader's influence was all the more impressive because, aside from the AFL-CIO, there were virtually no other consumer lobbyists in the sixties. The Consumer Federation of America (which included 140 individual groups) was not founded until 1967, and only in 1969 did the National Consumer Union establish an office in Washington.

Other consumer efforts instigated by Ralph Nader led to passage of the Child Protection Act in 1966, which banned dangerous toys, and the 1967 Flammable Fabrics Act. The latter followed testimony from Dr. Abraham Bergman, a Seattle pediatrician, who told Senator Warren Magnuson about the steady stream of burned and scarred children he had seen at the Seattle Children's Hospital. He urged Congress to mandate children's clothing, especially sleepwear, that was flame-resistant. CBS newsman Peter Hackes testified that his eleven-year-old daughter had been seriously burned when her cotton blouse caught on fire, even though it met all current safety standards. A similar act had become law in 1953, but it had set low standards and failed to cover such items as baby blankets, bedding, drapes, carpets, and upholstery fabrics.

The cotton textile industry massed in opposition to the Flammable Fabrics Bill, threatening Congress that "blood would run in the halls" before such legislation passed. But the industry seriously misjudged congressional and public sentiment. After only two days of hearings, the bill went to the Senate floor where it passed easily by voice vote. Although discussion in the House was more spirited, the bill emerged virtually unscathed (though it exempted all fabrics labeled for export) and received President Johnson's signature in December 1967. It extended the 1953 law to cover all wearing apparel and interior furnishings made of fabrics or related materials. After signing the measure, the president warned that "women are tired of meat with worms in it, blouses that burn, and pipe lines that blow up under their homes." LBJ had boarded the consumer bandwagon.

Perhaps the most important proconsumer acts to emerge from the Johnson administration, because of their broad scope and long-term implications, were the President's Commission on Consumer Interests and the Consumer Advisory Council, along with the National Commission on Product Safety. LBJ created the first two groups by executive order in January 1964, marking the first time in history that American consumers had direct representation in the White House. Business interests complained, but the public strongly supported these efforts. In 1967 the president requested that Congress form a National Commission on Product Safety. The legislation received swift approval. Comprised of seven members, the commission was charged not only to review products to determine their safety but to study whether existing laws adequately protected consumers. In remarks at the signing ceremonies, Johnson recited a litany of accident statistics before concluding that this "adds up to saying that we have lived too dangerously too long." Americans lived "each day and each hour surrounded by a great many hazards that we know nothing about." It was time for a change.

In a speech to the Consumer Assembly in Washington that November, LBJ proclaimed that "this is a consumer's administration" and cited his support for legislation that "materially helped consumers to a better life." This included not only acts protecting children and promoting automobile and highway safety, but a truth-in-packaging bill. Congress passed the measure in 1966 after five years of hearings, establishing standards for package information and identification and encouraging industry to develop standard package sizes. As LBJ later gloated, "The days of the 'jumbo-quart' and the 'giant economy quart' are already over."

Pushed by Michigan Democratic Senator Philip Hart and designed to make comparison shopping easier, the truth-in-packaging legislation encountered strong opposition from industry representatives. Charles Mortimer of General Foods led the attack, urging Congress to "keep politics out of the pantry." The proposal, he argued, tampered with "the machinery of free competition" and implied that food manufacturers took advantage of consumers through deception. Casting himself as the defender of "free choice," Mortimer attacked Esther Peterson and all consumer advocates as threats to the free-enterprise system. Theodore Gamble of the Pet Milk Company chimed in with claims that "consumers want different packaging because it adds interest and variety to their shopping and because it has values to them over and above the mere containment of a product." Despite support from the National Association of Manufacturers, the Chamber of Commerce, and the Grocery Manufacturers Association, the attack failed in the face of strong public support and a scathing critique of the industry published in *Consumer Reports*. Speaking about the law's impact on the cosmetics industry, Representative Leonor Sullivan of Missouri warned that this "is an area in which every woman—every woman—had better begin to play politics in every way she knows how, because your skin and your hair and your nails and your eyebrows and your lips and even your lives may be at stake some day."

A parallel measure, the Truth-in-Lending bill, offers perhaps the best example of the lack of consumer rights at the outset of the sixties and the glacial pace of change before 1966. First introduced in the spring of 1960, the legislation did not regulate credit but mandated the disclosure of total finance costs and actual annual interest rates for loans. At the time, banks and other loan institutions calculated interest in a variety of ways, leaving consumers to figure out charges and interest rates. Led by the National Retail Merchants Association, which argued that the bill "propagates fear, doubt, and distrust," retail merchants and banks opposed it. Stating a 1.5 percent monthly charge as an 18 percent annual interest rate (which, of course, it was), said one spokesman, "would create an undesirable psychological effect on the American consumer's buying habits, resulting in a serious business lag."

President Johnson asked for truth-in-lending legislation in November 1967 when he signed the bill establishing the National Consumer Product Safety Commission. "We need to crack down on the con man, the gyp who preys on the aged and who preys on the defenseless," he argued. The Senate passed the measure 92 to 0 in 1967, but the bill failed to reach the House floor before adjournment. The House took up the bill early the following year and passed it overwhelmingly (383 to 4). A conference report produced a strong bill, and the president signed it on May 29, 1968, eight years after it had first been introduced.

Consumer protection, Lyndon Johnson found, was a consensus issue that made no significant demands on the federal budget. Between 1964 and 1969, consequently, seventeen consumer protection laws passed Congress, though many Great Society efforts in this field proved to be more significant in the long run than they did at the moment of passage. That so many of these measures took years to become law reflected not only industry opposition but the slow emergence of a consumer consciousness throughout the 1960s. A few of the measures originated in the Kennedy years, but the Johnson effort laid the groundwork for the emergence of "consumers' rights" in the 1970s and after.

The late sixties was a time of strong antibusiness sentiment in the United States. Surveys of college students found few interested in business careers. Only 63 of 1,091 students in the Harvard class of 1966 went to work in the for-profit sector, and only 10 percent of the Columbia University class of 1967 were interested in a business career. A 1969 survey by industry insiders at *Fortune* magazine found that 94 percent of the students interviewed believed that "business was too profit-blinded and not concerned with public welfare." Ralph Nader's children were making their mark.

When industry discovered that the public not only supported consumer legislation but demanded it, they launched massive lobbying campaigns to prevent congressional action. During the Johnson years it was evident in such legislation as the Federal Cigarette and Labeling Advertising Act, passed in 1965. The American Cancer Society had urged the government to outline the link between smoking and cancer. In January 1964 a scientific report unanimously concluded that smoking caused lung cancer, chronic bronchitis, emphysema, and heart disease. Faced with intense lobbying by the tobacco industry, Congress retreated from significant regulation of cigarettes and required only that packages and cartons carry a health-hazard warning statement. It also expressly prohibited any other health warning requirements for at least four years and forbade the Federal Trade Commission from restricting cigarette advertising for five years.

Closely related to rising consumerism were new laws to promote beautification and environmental protection. Almost all of them increased government regulatory supervision, but they enjoyed broad public support and met little sustained opposition from the business community. By and large they targeted environmental pollution, and new federal requirements for such things as cleaner air and water initially brought with them funding to alleviate the costs of change.

Concern about beautification and environmental issues traced its popular appeal to the 1962 publication of Rachel Carson's best-selling *Silent Spring*. Carson described the danger of pesticides to wildlife and the nation's health, raising public consciousness. Soon thereafter residents on Long Island and in Michigan and Wisconsin tried to restrict the use of DDT, which caused birds' eggs to thin and then break before hatching. Carson's disclosures also boosted traditional groups like the Sierra Club and the National Wildlife Federation, which had long fought to preserve the country's natural resources. By 1967 the Audubon Society had established an Environmental Defense Fund to protect the environment through litigation. The short-term result of *Silent Spring* was passage of legislation directed at two specific targets: pollution and the preservation of the natural landscape.

In February 1965 Lyndon Johnson delivered the first presidential message ever devoted to natural beauty. "We have always prided ourselves on being not only America the strong and America the free," he told Congress, "but America the beautiful." A growing population and continued neglect of the nation's resources jeopardized that image. "The water we drink, the food we eat, the air we breathe," he warned, "are threatened with pollution." Parks and beaches were over-crowded; the wilderness was disappearing, and once gone it would not reappear. The president urged Congress to "act to prevent an ugly America." He proposed a battery of programs to remedy these ills, including highway beautification, clean-air and clean-water legislation, a White House conference on the issue, and a "parks-for-America decade."

"Beautification" served as a symbolic umbrella for these ini-tiatives, expressing a clear commitment to "an environment that is pleasing to the senses and healthy to live in." Although two decades later beautification advocates would attack ef-forts to regulate billboard advertising as a cruel illusion of progress, in 1965 these measures heralded a remarkable change in the outdoor aesthetics of the nation. Congress, how-ever, had no special enthusiasm for the new legislation, and it languished amid concerns over costs and funding. Spear-headed by Lady Bird Johnson (it became known as "Lady Bird's Bill" or, as Republican Melvin Laird sarcastically called it, "the President's wife's bill"), the Highway Beautification Act of 1965 eventually passed Congress and went to the presi-dent for his signature in mid-October. Although it attacked visual pollution, it was not a strong bill, in part because the Outdoor Advertising Association of America (which had hired a Johnson family attorney) helped shape its provisions. The legislation required junkyards to be cleaned up or screened, and regulated billboards along interstate highways. States that failed to comply would lose federal highway funds. A year later, however, Republicans narrowly missed deleting all funding for the program, and by fiscal years 1968 and 1969 they had the votes and eliminated funding authorization for beautification efforts.

More important was the effort to clean up the nation's

water supply. Congress turned back Texas Senator John Tower's attempt to deny any authority the right to "promulgate standards of water quality." Behind the leadership of Maine Democrat Edmund Muskie, it then passed the Water Quality Act of 1965 to prevent water pollution at its source rather than after it occurred downstream. The measure represented a vast improvement over the Water Pollution Control Act of 1948 and its later revisions. The 1948 act had vested full responsibility to control pollution with the states; the federal government provided only money and technical assistance. Now the government became more aggressive. The 1965 act still required the states to set standards, but they had to be approved by the Department of Health, Education and Welfare. (After its creation in 1970, the Environmental Protection Agency enforced the act.) This vested ultimate enforcement power with the federal government. The bill also provided financial incentives to states and municipalities through grants to improve sewage treatment facilities. When he signed the bill, President Johnson pledged to reopen the Potomac River for swimming by 1975, though he admitted that "bolder legislation" was needed in the years ahead.

A year later Congress overwhelmingly passed the Clean Water Restoration Act. This significantly increased federal funds to implement the 1965 act and authorized $3.9 billion over the next five years for states that complied with the earlier legislation. It also promised more research and removed funding restrictions for individual projects. Finally, in what turned out to be a significant step, it amended the 1924 Oil Pollution Act by requiring negligent companies to remove oil spills in navigable waters immediately. Although neither of these acts reversed the declining quality of the nation's water supplies, they did mark a commitment to change. Later, when a broader environmental consciousness seized the public in the 1970s, new legislation built on these early efforts.

Along with the water Americans drank, the quality of the air they breathed sparked concern. In 1963 Congress had enacted a Clean Air Act, and in 1965 and 1967 it amended and strengthened its provisions. The 1963 act was the first measure seriously to address air pollution. Although prevention of pollution remained the responsibility of state and local governments, the federal government now provided financial aid. The 1965 amendments particularly addressed the issue of motor vehicle emissions, which caused 40 to 60 percent of the country's air pollution, and provided for federal regulation through standards of emission for gasoline-powered vehicles. California and some other states had already moved in this direction, but the automotive industry wanted further delay of implementation. Placing responsibility for setting and enforcing standards at the federal level gave proponents of regulation more leverage, and the next several years saw a battle among regulators, industry representatives, and politicians to carve out compromises.

The 1967 Air Quality Act established the outlines of a nationwide program to control air pollution. The chief responsibility for setting and enforcing standards remained with the states, however, and the act failed to establish national emission standards as the president had requested. The federal government, through HEW, created air quality control regions in the country, published criteria for individual pollutants, and was supposed to help states establish their own programs. If they failed to do so, the federal government threatened to intervene. Air quality did improve somewhat during the next several years. Levels of particulate matter (dust and soot) fell by almost 20 percent by 1970, and airborne sulfur dioxide declined by almost 60 percent during the same period.

Like earlier measures to control water and air pollution, the 1967 act was not an exercise in structural reform. None of these acts authorized federal intervention to prevent the causes of air pollution, only to eliminate it after the fact. In a sign of future battles, the coal industry swiftly attacked the Public Health Service's first report on the health effects of sulfur oxides in 1967. American industry diligently resisted effective legislation to prevent pollution. More sweeping (and effective) control measures awaited a broader public awakening to the problem.

Indicative of what remained to be done was the problem of beer and soft-drink containers. Americans used and discarded millions of them annually; recycling was virtually unheard of. Initial efforts to address this issue began with the 1965 passage of the Solid Waste Disposal Act. But this was really an offshoot of the concern about air and water pollution, and authorized funds only for research, training, and planning at the state level. It failed to establish federal regulations or funds for the construction of solid-waste facilities.

The other major thrust of Great Society environmental legislation, led chiefly by Secretary of the Interior Stewart Udall, was the preservation of natural resources. Four major legislative initiatives spearheaded the attack: the Wilderness Act of 1964, the Land and Water Conservation Fund Act of 1965, the National Wild and Scenic Rivers Act of 1968, and the National Trails Act of 1968. Of these, the Wilderness Act was particularly important because it authorized the involvement of citizens' groups in formulating proposals. This gave the growing number of conservation and preservation groups access to the legislative process and virtually guaranteed stronger environmental protection legislation in the future. In

November 1966 President Johnson appointed a Task Force on Environmental Health and Related Problems to explore these issues further. The title of its 1967 report, *A Strategy for a Livable Environment,* sounded a theme that dominated the next decade. In 1968 the president appointed a commission headed by Julius Stratton of the Ford Foundation to promote the management of coastal-zone resources.

Before he left office in January 1969, President Johnson signed almost three hundred measures involving beautification and conservation. These not only recognized but stimulated public support for environmental protection and the preservation of what Interior Secretary Stewart Udall called "a rich outdoor heritage." Environmentalist Edward Abbey later wrote, "Wilderness is not a luxury but a necessity of the human spirit." Amid a decade beset by urban ills, Americans more than ever sought refuge in nature. National parks and seashores became popular vacation destinations, so popular that by the 1980s vacationers and sightseers overwhelmed their facilities and threatened to destroy the very environment the parks were designed to preserve. Nowhere was the problem-oriented politics of the Great Society more evident than in the rise of environmental politics and a revived concept of the public interest. These not only survived the decade, they gathered strength when other Great Society reforms withered. By the 1980s they triggered a backlash from mine owners, lumber companies, ranchers, and developers. Environmental law became a hotbed of controversy during the Reagan administration and beyond.

A related quality-of-life effort of the Great Society, one that also became embroiled in controversy by the 1980s, was the promotion of national cultural life. In 1964 a Commission on the Humanities, chaired by Brown University President Barnaby Kenney, recommended the creation of a National Humanities Foundation similar to the National Science Foundation. President Johnson supported the proposal, first in a 1964 speech at Brown and again in his 1965 State of the Union Message. By January 1965 more than seventy bills had been introduced in Congress to promote the arts as well as the humanities.

Kenney believed that "our fulfillment as a nation depends upon the development of our minds, and our relations to one another and to our society depend upon our understanding of one another and our society." The arts and humanities were at the "center of our lives," he insisted. Republican Congressman Frank Horton of New York echoed this theme, arguing that "revitalization of the humanities can be an antidote to the fading image of individuals increasingly obscured in a contemporary world of 'bigness.'" Pennsylvania Democrat William Moorhead went further, citing the need to "inspire the education of generalists who can understand and articulate the critical values that give compelling meaning and a sense of direction to human life. . . ."

In March 1965 the Rockefeller Brothers Fund released a report on "The Performing Arts: Problems and Prospects," recommending a broad program of federal, state, and local support for the arts. Arts councils, touring companies, and favorable tax treatment were essential, the report argued, if the arts were to flourish in the United States. When House-Senate hearings began soon thereafter, the Johnson administration finally submitted its own bill. Leadership in this effort fell to Rhode Island Senator Claiborne Pell. In a 1964 speech before the National Society of Arts and Letters, Pell underlined the major issue: "We are in conflict today with the materialism of totalitarian forms of government, which by definition stifle creative thought. We must contribute to the world something better than this, something more lofty, something in tune with freemen, something to inspire them."

Tying the nation's cultural enhancement to the competitive juices of the cold war inspired Congress to act. A few conservatives, such as Strom Thurmond of South Carolina, objected on grounds that this was a misuse of federal power and federal funds and worried that the government would try to control the arts. (By the 1980s Thurmond and his conservative colleagues were able to do just that themselves.) Pell countered by insisting that the "Federal Government has a vital role to play in the fostering of the central, the basic cultural values in American life."

In that spirit, Congress in 1965 established a National Foundation on the Arts and Humanities. It consisted of two autonomous bodies, a National Endowment for the Humanities and a National Endowment for the Arts. Each agency had its own chair and advisory board and could make grants for a wide range of activities. To encourage private donations, most grants depended on matching funds.

A related endeavor was the Corporation for Public Broadcasting, a nonprofit, nongovernmental body. Created in 1967 by the Public Broadcasting Act, it stemmed from a 1967 report by the Carnegie Commission on Educational Television. The legislation provided financial aid for educational broadcasting but was controversial because of fears that governmental or political pressures would influence programming. These fears persisted, and long-term funding was never secure. The emergence of PBS was significant, however, not only because it promoted high-quality programming in the arts and humanities but because it also offered nationwide educational programming. Persistent struggles to control or influence the content of its programs were testimony to its public appeal.

LBJ's Great Society also addressed the issue of crime. Clearly different from other efforts to elevate Americans' quality of life, by 1967 and 1968 the crime issue symbolized the declining hopes of the Great Society. Several "hot" summers of urban rioting, a sharply polarized nation, a backlash against administration domestic and foreign policies, steadily rising racial tensions, and critics' dismay at the failure of Great Society programs to quickly solve the nation's problems all led to a hauntingly pessimistic mood. The crime issue was not new; concern had paralleled rising crime rates from 1960 to 1965. But the emergence of a backlash candidate in George Wallace, whose 1968 presidential campaign emphasized crime and disorder, further focused public attention.

LBJ established the President's Commission on Law Enforcement and the Administration of Justice in 1965 to study the causes of crime and suggest measures to prevent it. Two years later, in a vastly changed political atmosphere, it issued a report: "The Challenge of Crime in a Free Society." The report argued that the "existence of crime, the talk about crime, the reports of crime, and the fear of crime have eroded the basic quality of life of many Americans." Almost half of those interviewed said that fear of crime kept them off the streets at night, and 20 percent said they would like to move to a different neighborhood. The commission linked the growth of crime to "increasing urbanization" of the country and the "increasing numerousness, restlessness, and restiveness of American youth." It also lamented the apparent decline of parental authority, with an accompanying fall in moral standards.

The report concluded that social action was essential to the prevention of crime, and endorsed the Great Society's efforts to fight poverty, educate children, and rebuild cities: "Reducing poverty, discrimination, ignorance, disease and urban blight, and the anger, cynicism or despair those conditions can inspire, is one great step toward reducing crime." It characterized the justice system as "undernourished" and called for more manpower, training, facilities, and equipment. The commission also warned that despite public fears, much crime was relatively minor. One of every three arrests in the country during 1965, for example, had been for public drunkenness. This was a far cry from popular images of rampant criminal behavior in the form of urban arson or wanton murder.

Although the public focused more sharply on crime in the late 1960s, Congress had been trying to pass crime bills for the District of Columbia since the late 1950s. A 1966 law died when President Johnson pocket-vetoed it. In 1967, however, Congress finally succeeded. The so-called District of Columbia Crime Bill was important as a harbinger of tougher public attitudes toward crime as well as an indicator of growing fear for the quality of life in the country. Particularly noteworthy were its punitive sanctions. The bill authorized warrantless arrests and investigative detention, added penalties for inciting riots, increased mandatory minimum sentences, labeled obstruction of justice a crime, and toughened obscenity laws.

The key measure in the new war on crime was the Omnibus Crime Control and Safe Streets Act (later renamed the Law Enforcement and Criminal Justice Assistance Act), proposed in 1967 and highlighted by LBJ in February 1968 in a special message on crime. This bill offered the most sweeping anticrime legislation in history; by endorsing it the president hoped to avoid being labeled "soft on crime." Despite its punitive features, it also reflected LBJ's conviction that crime was in part environmental. Congress did not share that perspective and moved instead to curtail citizens' rights and invade personal privacy in the name of fighting crime.

Eventually passed by Congress in 1968, the law's very emphasis on "safe streets" reflected the growing fear of crime in American culture amid recent urban violence. It focused on the prevention and control of civil disorders and sought to upgrade state and local police forces and courts for that purpose. Despite congressional concern, an insignificant $125 million was budgeted to fund the program nationwide. Somewhat paradoxically, the president also proposed to outlaw electronic surveillance, even though FBI and military intelligence covert activities were becoming a key ingredient in fighting crime (among their other, often illegal, uses, such as the FBI's COINTELPRO efforts against dissident groups). Congress rejected efforts to curtail wiretapping and tried to overturn Supreme Court decisions supporting the rights of defendants. The climate that produced the Safe Streets Act reflected the popularity of punitive measures as a response to urban and social distress. Election-year political considerations led the president to sign the measure.

By the time Lyndon Johnson left office in January 1969, earlier presumptions that the United States was entering a postscarcity society where economic affluence would lead to social harmony had long since disappeared. Domestic dissent, deepening division over the war in Vietnam, and a growing concern about inflation led many Americans to question the inevitability of economic growth. Yet even as they challenged the assumptions that had fueled the quality-of-life theme, they continued to embrace its major goals. Clean air, clean water, a healthy environment, protection against corporate wrongdoing, and greater "truth" in consumer issues remained vibrant concerns. Indeed, in the following decades consumer consciousness increased even when political support for government regulation declined. Consumerism became one of the most persistent features of the last third of the twentieth century.

6

Assessing the Great Society

LYNDON JOHNSON announced in March 1968 that he would not run for reelection. He left the White House in January 1969 after five years as president, his Great Society not only stalled but under attack. In the ensuing years Republicans, conservatives, and even liberals have criticized Great Society legislation as misguided, flawed, dangerous, and often a total failure. One survey of newspaper articles found a pattern of critical commentary from 1968 to 1988. At first complaints focused on administrative and fiscal concerns. After the mid-1970s they shifted to blame Great Society legislation for the economic problems of that decade, and by the 1980s they argued that the legislation itself had caused most of the social problems then plaguing American society. In the process, critics drew little distinction between Great Society legislation and later legislative efforts to expand, contract, or refine LBJ's programs.

In these later years the liberalism so politically attractive and powerful in the mid-sixties fell victim to internal doubts as well as conservative attacks. The 1960s now seem an unusual decade, one that may not (some say should not) be repeated ever again. And the years from 1964 to 1966, when the bulk of the Great Society legislation became law, appear even more unique. They represent a liberal interlude unmatched in the twentieth century, except perhaps for the mid-1930s, and unlikely to recur in the foreseeable future. After 1966 the Congress became more conservative, more preoccupied with punishing "disorderly" individuals than with eradicating the causes of their discontents.

This change in the national mood is the first thing to re-member in assessing the Great Society. To assume that what-ever happened after the Great Society stemmed from its legislation is to confuse chronology with causation. Critics argue that LBJ's "wrongheaded" legislative initiatives and ex-cessive use of federal funds bear the responsibility for deterio-rating urban conditions and rising welfare rolls (to take just two examples). They would be at least as correct to argue that later problems were due to underfunding, the narrow scope of Great Society legislation, or the law of unintended conse-quences. The dramatic shift in American social life between the mid-1960s and the mid-1980s has yet to be fully understood.

Race played a central role in the Great Society's accomplish-ments and failings. The civil rights movement brought race out of the closet and forced Americans to confront its implica-tions directly. Many Americans then discovered they sup-ported racial equality in theory but objected to its operation in practice. All Great Society legislation, of course, was not re-lated to race, but for most issues that question infused discus-sions and shaped responses. Welfare in particular became identified with race, and since many Great Society programs were means-tested (based on financial eligibility) they became tied to welfare in the public consciousness and often in fact.

The confusion of culture and cultural politics with issues of economics and class also shapes our assessment of the Great Society. A sexual revolution, widespread use of recreational drugs, the growing women's movement, protest against the war in Vietnam—all questioned traditional values in the 1960s and challenged Americans to change. Conservatives seized on these phenomena to discredit liberalism and its products, including the Great Society. Many critiques, such as those of Newt Gingrich noted earlier, stem from questions of culture and "values." The so-called Reagan Democrats of the 1980s found values questions (such as abortion or premarital sex) more compelling than economic issues. In addition, as the changing economic climate ended boundless horizons of limitless growth, politicians used cultural issues—such as family nurture or racial discrimination—to avoid questions of economics and class in explaining persistent poverty.

To assess each of the major themes of the Great Society in detail would require at least another book. In the years since 1968, not only has our understanding of the problems it addressed become more complex, federal efforts to address them have become far more complicated. Debates have often focused as much on ideology and political posturing as they have on substantive matters. A brief glance at the intervening years, however, can help put the efforts of the Great Society in perspective.

Few would object that civil rights was a compelling success story. Passage of the 1964 Civil Rights Act and the Voting Rights Act of 1965, along with later civil rights legislation, changed the patterns of race relations and political power in the United States in a way not likely to be reversed. When the debate turned from civil rights to race in the late sixties, the white public reacted sharply. Although the effect was to blame the Great Society, legislative initiatives had less to do with this backlash than the changing cultural ethos. Black Power was an indigenous outpouring of militancy that substituted the rhetoric of race for that of civil rights. Its major impact was to bring the Great Society to a screeching halt as white support for racial change evaporated in the face of riots and continued demonstrations. The dissolution of the civil rights coalition symbolized the deterioration of the consensus upon which the Great Society rested.

As much as racial militancy antagonized whites, the shift in the proof of discrimination—from unequal treatment, with its emphasis on opportunity, to unequal impact, with its focus on outcome—created a racial wedge that frustrated efforts to reinvigorate the earlier idealism of civil rights. This results-based emphasis, popularly known as affirmative action, ran contrary to provisions in the 1964 Civil Rights Act and represented frustration at that act's inability to remedy racial discrimination quickly. Supreme Court decisions in *Griggs v. Duke Power Co.* (1970) and *Swann v. Charlotte-Mecklenburg County School District* (1971) reinforced affirmative action as the appropriate remedy for continued discrimination. The *Griggs* case embraced the unequal-impact theory, and the *Swann* case held that school busing to achieve racial integration was constitutional.

This shift in emphasis from opportunity to results, as well as the increased racial militancy and urban riots of the late sixties, provoked not only obstinate white resistance to further civil rights legislation but a conviction that the movement had gone too far. In the years after 1970, as Republican administrations came to power largely on the strength of white votes, and as the Republican party gained strength in the white South, racial antagonisms simmered throughout the country. By the 1990s race, not civil rights, clearly characterized the issue of discrimination. Both sides often talked past, not at, each other. With that in mind, in 1997 President Bill Clinton called for a national dialogue on race.

Despite this continuing conundrum of race, without question the most controversial assessments of the Great Society lie in the area of antipoverty legislation. Specifically, did the Great Society alleviate poverty? Or did the legislation merely give the poor a sense that relief was a "right" and thereby inflate the welfare rolls? There are probably as many answers as there are questions. We do know that from 1965 to 1969 the number of people officially in poverty declined, from about 17 percent of the population to approximately 12 percent. But was this the result of antipoverty legislation or economic growth? Certainly economic growth accounted for a portion of the shift, but only about 3 percent according to most estimates. Then, when the economy turned sour in the 1970s and 1980s, much of that growth was lost. The point is that government transfer programs, not economic growth, removed many individuals from poverty. Conservative arguments that free-market economics could cure poverty proved hallucinatory.

Central in criticism of the antipoverty effort is the Community Action Program and its Community Action Agencies. Intended to increase local decision-making and facilitate the "maximum feasible participation" of those most affected by new programs, the CAPs and CAAs proved problematic precisely because they threatened real change. They challenged existing power structures and aroused opposition from entrenched political interests, many of them tied to the Democratic party. Their potential for change was real because they promised to empower the powerless. Along with Legal Services, they exposed a fundamental flaw in Great Society antipoverty legislation. Where it promised to alleviate problems, it hoped to do so simply by increasing the size of the pie. The provision of services replaced systemic or structural change. The left attacked LBJ for this limited vision; the right opposed him for having it in the first place.

Among the most significant influences on the poverty issue

have been the changing nature of the American economy since the 1960s and the shifting perception of the problem. New technologies have flourished and older industries have decayed or disappeared. This has eliminated a "safety valve" for unskilled or semiskilled workers, or workers with limited educational experience, who previously found employment in the mass-production industries so important since the late nineteenth century. Once workers lost their postscarcity visions, the politics of scarcity returned with a vengeance, and working-class Americans believed that what helped one group hurt another. They quickly lost all enthusiasm for change. As economic conditions worsened during the ensuing decades, social policy unraveled.

Coupled with this development was a significant shift in the focus of antipoverty discussions. As Michael Katz has argued, at the beginning of the decade the focus was on the white poor in rural areas. After 1964 it shifted to concentrate on African Americans in the cities. This injected race into the debates and significantly altered public support for antipoverty measures. It also obscured the reality that most social welfare spending, such as Social Security, was not limited to the poor, and it directed attention away from an underlying characteristic of poverty, its transitory nature.

After 1968 the Great Society's antipoverty program found itself in the hands of its opponents. With the exception of Jimmy Carter, Republicans controlled the White House for the next quarter-century. Even Carter, a conservative Democrat, rejected the federal activism of the sixties. But poverty would not disappear, and chief executives after Lyndon Johnson grappled with the problem in various ways.

Richard Nixon at first expanded antipoverty efforts. By 1975 social welfare spending as a percentage of total federal expenditures had risen substantially. Between 1970 and 1972 alone it almost doubled. Even Nixon's fiscal 1974 budget requested 58 percent more money (in constant dollars) for social programs than Lyndon Johnson had in his final year. Nixon's chief effort to restructure the system, the Family Assistance Plan, failed to pass Congress. But later efforts (such as the 1971 Work Incentive Program) illustrated Nixon's determination to increase work incentives and strengthen the structure of the family. Both efforts reflected the influence of Daniel Patrick Moynihan. The other attempt to alleviate poverty during the Nixon years was his proposal of a negative income tax. It was designed to help the working poor and reflected Nixon's concern that welfare penalized work. Nixon, as well as his successor Gerald Ford, accepted the outlines of a national welfare state. Even a conservative like Ford proposed only to reduce the rate of growth of those programs.

The Carter years marked a conservative backlash among Democrats as well as Republicans. After 1976 means-tested programs failed to grow. More rigid bureaucratic rules accompanied cuts in benefits. Carter was a fiscal conservative who rejected not only the specifics but the philosophy of the Great Society. He declared as much when he presented his 1979 budget to Congress: "Government cannot eliminate poverty or provide a bountiful economy or reduce inflation or save our cities or cure illiteracy or provide energy."

By the time Ronald Reagan entered the White House, a conservative ideology dominated discussions of antipoverty and welfare. According to that ideology, the poor deserved their fate, and efforts to provide welfare were therefore a waste of money. Work incentives and the removal of individuals from the welfare rolls became the administration's chief priorities. Beginning in 1981 with the Omnibus Budget Reconciliation Act, welfare programs were cut back. Later, through what it called the "New Federalism," the administration tried to shift responsibility for welfare to the states. From 1986 to 1988, debates raged over how best to reform welfare, partially in response to a sudden upsurge in poverty rates between 1978 and 1983. A Tax Reform Act in 1986 removed most poor families from the tax rolls through various changes in the tax code. But benefit levels continued to decline and incomes stagnated. Then, in 1988, Congress passed the Family Support Act. This emphasized "work, child support and need-based family support supplements" in an effort to eliminate "long-term welfare dependency." At the end of the 1980s welfare spending was lower in real terms than at the beginning of the 1970s, with real AFDC spending less than one-third its former size. The Reagan efforts rested on the assumption that the real problem was as much individuals' moral fiber as it was the economic structure of society.

By the early 1990s the face of welfare had changed. Most AFDC recipients were young single mothers with one or two children, not (as in 1973) divorced or separated from a husband and the children's father. Still, public images of poverty remained firmly fixed on African Americans, despite the fact that 67 percent of the nation's poor in 1997 were white. Stereotyping too often substituted for analysis in public discussions of the issue. The Clinton administration's policies resembled those of his Republican predecessors, emphasizing work incentives and allowing individual states to experiment with various programs to move families off welfare. Congress passed a stringent welfare reform bill that curbed eligibility for welfare benefits nationwide. Even with the elixir of healthy economic growth, however, government seemed at best able only to alleviate rather than eradicate poverty in the United States.

The health and education policies of the Great Society occasioned controversy over process more than goals. The central issue in education, aid to parochial schools, was resolved before the 1965 acts passed. Aside from lingering debates over the content of instruction and a tolerable level of federal intrusiveness, most subsequent educational controversies have involved race. School integration, busing in particular, has aroused concerns about federal power (often couched in terms of "the neighborhood school") and the strings attached to federal monies for education. But most communities have taken the funds; indeed, most urban school districts have become dangerously dependent on federal funds for essential programs. Federal budgetary concerns, rather than programmatic issues, have led critics to argue for retrenchment. The chief controversies, from the 1970s to the 1990s, remained those of school integration, federal power, and student assistance programs.

The health care debates have been quite different. Despite a growing awareness about the depth and breadth of the health care crisis, until the federal programs of the mid-sixties few reliable statistics documented the limited access of many citizens to quality health care. Once recognized, this problem quickly led to budgetary debates over affordability, delivery of services, and rising health care costs. The rapid development and proliferation of new health care technologies exacerbated the problem, causing cost containment and quality care to seem mutually exclusive.

The American Medical Association successfully opposed national health care. Polls indicated, on the other hand, that most Americans supported some form of federally sponsored program but wanted to retain their personal physicians and choose their services. This contradictory mix, together with the turbulent and cash-rich politics of health care, forestalled any significant overhaul of the system. Expenses for Medicare and Medicaid rose astronomically amid expanding utilization and some fraud, but demands for cost control and opposition to fraud produced no clear answers. The budget share for spending on social welfare, education, and health care doubled between 1965 and 1980, with a growth rate (12 percent) that was twice that of the economy as a whole.

The central health care issue from 1968 into the late 1990s was that of national health insurance. In 1977, when Jimmy Carter took office, 40 million Americans had little or no medical coverage. By 1992 38.9 million Americans still were without medical insurance at some time during the year. Compounding this issue was the problem of spiraling medical and hospital costs throughout the three decades following passage of Medicare and Medicaid. As early as 1967 Congress had enacted legislation to limit Medicare spending, and in 1972 it allowed states to charge premiums to Medicaid patients. Professional Standards Review Organizations, created in 1972, also tried to hold down costs by monitoring the quality and quantity of care. Still medical costs rose steadily. The Reagan administration eventually tried to limit hospital costs through a 1983 Social Security reform measure.

During the 1980s programs such as Medicaid expanded their patient population significantly, enrolling more than 35 million people by 1992. Most of this expansion occurred as a result of annual budget provisions during the Reagan years and embraced chiefly children and pregnant women. Costs rose too, especially in the 1980s. But the rise in costs was somewhat deceptive. Two-thirds of all cost increases occurred for two groups of patients, the elderly and the blind and disabled, though three-quarters of all patients were adults and children. Medicare also attracted the attention of budget cutters. Every Reagan and Bush budget proposed significant cuts in Medicare, and Congress passed many of them. Nonetheless annual growth exceeded the size of any spending cuts. The problem with Medicare has been primarily one of costs; since its expansion to include end-stage renal disease and disabled persons in 1972, it has not been extended to any broad new group. This exemplifies the shift from access to cost containment.

Compounding efforts to deal with the health care issue was the rapidly changing nature of health care delivery in the United States. The emergence of Health Maintenance Organizations, as well as an assortment of other employer-driven cost-containment measures, left consumers bewildered and afraid that change meant the erosion of their medical benefits. Perhaps the primary impact of these changes has been a change in payment philosophy, from one based on "reasonable costs" to one that rests on predetermined prices. In all, consumers' fear of change, the incredibly complex issues of medical care, and the political volatility of the issue have led to paralysis. Efforts by the Clinton administration in the early 1990s to put together a health care reform package fell victim to all three factors.

Urban problems have seemed equally complex and resistant to change. In large part this is because they embrace a host of interrelated issues: unemployment, racial discrimination, housing deterioration, job flight, white flight, lack of health care resources, limited educational opportunities. The synergistic effect of these phenomena has led, as William Julius Wilson has argued, to a "truly disadvantaged" class of individuals trapped in America's urban communities. For too many Americans the inner cities have become a graveyard for the promise of American life. By the 1980s electoral power had swung to the suburbs, whose residents had little interest in urban issues and focused on their own problems. Funding for most urban programs dried up, especially as conservatives (few of whom came from urban areas) gained power in Washington.

Finally, the Great Society's efforts to improve the quality of American life has become more popular as the years have passed. Later administrations, Republican and Democrat alike, extended the scope of these laws. By the 1980s Reagan administration attempts to repeal many of their provisions caused a public outcry. The middle class has firmly embraced environmental protection and consumer safeguards. Formal celebration of Earth Day, beginning in 1970, has symbolized this new public consciousness. As with the other Great Society programs, the millennium has not been reached. But water has become purer, as has the air; wildlife (such as the bald eagle) has made a dramatic comeback in areas where extinction seemed imminent; and public interest in safety standards for consumer products has persisted.

Quite apart from Great Society policies themselves is the question of their implementation. In almost every case political compromises were necessary to pass legislation. This is how the American political system works, but in time some of those compromises revealed legislative flaws. As Hugh Davis Graham has pointed out, too often delivery agencies significantly altered the intent and operation of the original legislation to promote their own agendas. Through "iron triangles" and the use of clientele capture, the very objects of Great Society reforms all too often seized control of the process to block significant change and enhance their own interests. Tied to this was the unwieldy structure of the federal government, which defied the handling of problems that cut across portions of the bureaucracy.

LBJ recognized this and appointed a businessman, Ben Heineman, to head a Task Force on Government Organization and suggest solutions. It recommended strengthening the executive office of the presidency, unifying departments and agencies into "superdepartments," and decentralizing regional administration. Due to report in late 1967, its major recommendations did not become public until the Nixon years.

Lyndon Johnson himself exacerbated many of these problems, often failing to develop advance support for his program among Democrats or the public at large. He not only attacked structural problems through reforms that left existing institutions intact, he implied that the public could support his legislative initiatives without fear of pain or of themselves being changed. Without a politically mobilized constituency, once the middle class retreated from its commitment to helping others, political support for Great Society programs evaporated. Add to this LBJ's penchant for secrecy, and what emerged was a policy mix that avoided public debate and was almost guaranteed to mislead and invite cynicism. LBJ, in short, mistook lack of debate for consensus government. It was, David Broder aptly noted, "hand-me-down government carried to its ultimate expression, with bounties, benefits, and, of course, directions issuing from the top." Writing his memoirs a few years later, the former president admitted as much:

> I tried to make it possible for every child of every color to grow up in a nice house, eat a solid breakfast, to attend a decent school and to get a good and lasting job. I asked so little in return, just a little thanks. Just a little appreciation. That's all. But look at what I got instead. Riots in 175 cities. Looting. Burning. Shooting. . . . Young people by the thousands leaving the university, marching in the streets, chanting that horrible song about how many kids I had killed that day. . . . It ruined everything.

Defenders of the Great Society had a different perspective. Richard Goodwin, one of its chief architects, claimed that it did not fail but was abandoned. The experiments of the first two years fell victim to the war in Vietnam, which induced divisiveness and budgetary difficulties. By the 1967 budget, almost 75 percent of funds were designated for war or war-related programs, with only 12.2 percent targeted for health, education, and welfare. After his first term, Richard Nixon abandoned most efforts at reform in an effort to save himself from the ravages of Watergate.

The Great Society failed to grow, as Johnson had hoped, into a "beautiful woman." LBJ had anticipated that his legislation would be "more permanent even than the New Deal." That it was not reflects the failure of Lyndon Johnson as much as (if not more than) the failure of a legislative program. Too often Johnson deliberately understated the continuing costs of new programs and requested only modest funding, hoping that once under way neither Congress nor the public would desert them. This led him to begin more programs than the bureaucracy, the public, or the budget could digest at one time. It also led him to overpromise, to insist that each new endeavor was not only essential but represented *the* solution to complex and perplexing problems. But laws are not an end in themselves. As White House aide Joseph Califano admitted, "We did not recognize that government could not do it all."

Budget Director Charles Schultze summarized this view in the fall of 1966 when he confessed that "*we are not able to fund adequately the new Great Society programs.*" But expectations continued to rise. "This leads," Schultze admitted, "to *frustration, loss of credibility, and even deterioration* of State and local services. . . . *Backlog, queuing,* and *griping* build up steadily." Without extensive debate, the public never understood just how complex or interrelated the problems were. While voters overwhelmingly approved LBJ's initiatives in 1965 and 1966, few understood that they represented a beginning rather than the final word. The Great Society, one writer noted, was an aspiration rather than a blueprint. It died when Americans replaced hope with cynicism.

Critics of the Great Society, however, often neglect its popularity and its bipartisanship. Despite controversies, debates, or political and ideological polarization, polls continue to indicate strong public support for these legislative objectives. A Harris Poll in the late 1970s revealed that 82 percent of respondents backed medical care for the aged (98 percent by the 1980s), 90 percent favored federal aid to education, and 95 percent supported the Voting Rights Act. Other polls in the 1980s produced similar results, with respondents supporting level or increased expenditures for these and other programs. Even 76 percent supported the food stamp program, which critics charged promoted welfare dependency. This suggests that the Great Society's objectives were widely accepted, if specific proposals to reach them sparked debate. Republican support for many Great Society measures reflects that acceptance. On several key measures—voting rights, water pollution, Medicare, education, manpower development, truth in packaging, auto safety—significant numbers of Republicans joined Democrats to pass legislation. Only a few bills—the creation of HUD, housing, antipoverty, highway beauty, Model Cities—attracted limited Republican support. From the perspective of the mid-1990s, however, it is clear that many of those Republicans were moderates or even liberals, the likes of which have since failed at reelection, left the party, or died.

Republicans' support for this legislation, and their replacement by individuals more narrowly committed to an ideological conservatism, reflects another element of the Great Society years that goes beyond legislative specifics to a broader essence. That is the question, defined best by Marshall Kaplan

and Peggy Cuciti, of a "national community." Before the polarization of the late 1960s and backlash politics, the "me
decade" of the 1970s, or the naked selfishness of the 1980s, a
commitment to a broader national community pervaded the
country. Now so very "sixties," and depicted as the embodi-
ment of the Woodstock Generation, this commitment muted
divisions of class and race. It recognized, Kaplan and Cuciti
concluded, "responsibility for improving the position of the
least advantaged and for shaping the quality of the physical
and social environments, its willingness to experiment and to
be evaluated and finally its trust in government as the lever for
achieving desired change."

Apart from changing priorities, shifting political fortunes,
and the movement of the American political spectrum to the
right, one other factor helps explain the mixed results of Great
Society legislation. Lloyd Ohlin, an architect of community
action, summed it up best: "I think we learned the enormous
resistance of these institutions to change, their tremendous capacity to resiliently absorb protest, aggression against them,
attempts to change their goals or directions, and the internal
distribution of power and responsibility within them. Wrong
analysis, wrong prescription, wrong results." The Great Society did not solve the problems it identified and addressed,
often for the reasons Ohlin suggested. But also missing, despite the rhetoric of a "war" on poverty or the creation of
"model" cities, was the national will to win the battles and
solve the problems whatever the cost. Much of this failure
seems rooted not in the Great Society or the personality of
Lyndon Johnson but in the national character. Americans remain more concerned to separate the "deserving" from the
"undeserving" poor than to eliminate poverty. Americans are
willing to sacrifice as individuals (the Peace Corps, VISTA,
Teach for America) but not as a community. The majority re-

main committed to a belief that all change should be moderate at best.

Embedded in American culture, at least since World War II, is a conviction that economic growth can solve most problems painlessly. If only we could find the correct policies for fine-tuning the economy, it would produce abundance for all. Assured of its future, the middle class would then allocate resources to the poor. We are a middle-class society, and this is both a strength and a weakness. On the one hand a broad middle class reflects the economic success of American capitalism. At the same time the mythic vision of that class leads it to credit itself for its success, and fear of falling prompts it to embrace miserly visions for those less fortunate when the economy slows. By the late 1970s this had led, in the words of civil rights activist Vernon Jordan, to a "new minimalism," which meant "fewer rights and freedoms for those on the bottom half of our social ladder."

When all is said and done, perhaps the biggest failure of Lyndon Johnson's Great Society, a failure shared by the public and critics alike, was its lack of understanding and appreciation for the challenges it confronted. Once Americans saw the scope of the task, its complexity and costs overwhelmed them. The problems remained, the debates continued; but with the consensus frayed, the economy in decline, and the social fabric apparently unraveling, the national will atrophied. In the words of the advocate John Gardner, "I see a society learning new ways as a baby learns to walk. He stands up, falls, stands again, falls and bumps his nose, cries, tries again—and eventually walks. Some of the critics now sounding off about the Great Society would stop the baby after his first fall and say, 'That'll teach you. Stick to crawling.' "

A Note on Sources

THIS BOOK draws on a wide range of published materials on the Great Society. While only a few can be noted here, several primary sources are particularly useful. The various congressional hearings for the major pieces of Great Society legislation convey the flavor and fervor of the times, as does the *Congressional Record*. The *Congressional Quarterly Almanac* (Washington, D.C., 1964–1968) provides concise summaries of leading debates and issues. The memoirs of several leading participants are also important: Joseph Califano, Jr., *The Triumph and Tragedy of Lyndon Johnson: The White House Years* (New York, 1991); Richard Goodwin, *Remembering America: A Voice from the Sixties* (Boston, 1988); and Lyndon Johnson, *The Vantage Point: Perspectives of the Presidency, 1963–1968* (New York, 1971). Recently released tapes at the Lyndon B. Johnson Library in Austin, Texas, provide not only the substance of policy formation but a sense of the Johnson presidency.

Two recent histories of the Johnson years that explore some of these themes but have larger purposes are Irving Bernstein, *Guns or Butter: The Presidency of Lyndon Johnson* (New York, 1996), and Irwin Unger, *The Best of Intentions: The Triumph and Failures of the Great Society Under Kennedy, Johnson, and Nixon* (New York, 1996). These supersede Vaughn Bornet's earlier study, *The Presidency of Lyndon Johnson* (Lawrence, Kans., 1983).

Other secondary studies that provide useful general commentary on the period are Paul Conkin, *Big Daddy from the Pedernales: Lyndon Baines Johnson* (New York, 1986); Gareth Davies, *From Opportunity to Entitlement: The Transformation and Decline of Great Society Liberalism* (Lawrence, Kans., 1996); Robert Divine, ed., *Exploring the Johnson Years* (Austin, Tex., 1981); Allen

Matusow, *The Unravelling of America: A History of Liberalism in the 1960s* (New York, 1984); Emmette Redford and Marlan Blissett, *Organizing the Executive Branch: The Johnson Presidency* (Chicago, 1981); James L. Sundquist, *Politics and Policy: The Eisenhower, Kennedy, and Johnson Years* (Washington, D.C., 1968); David C. Warner, ed., *Toward New Human Rights: The Social Policies of the Kennedy and Johnson Administrations* (Austin, Tex., 1977); and David Wellborn, *Regulation in the White House: The Johnson Presidency* (Austin, Tex., 1993). Like the sources that follow, many of these embrace multiple topics within a single volume. In the discussion below I have listed each source only once, placing it in the context where it provided me the most enlightenment.

INTRODUCTION

Any consideration of the background to the Great Society should begin with Emmette Redford and Richard McCulley, *White House Operations: The Johnson Presidency* (Austin, Tex., 1986). Also important are Bertram Gross, ed., *A Great Society?* (New York, 1966); Harry McPherson, *A Political Education* (Boston, 1972); and Hugh Sidey, *A Very Personal Presidency: Lyndon Johnson in the White House* (New York, 1968). More recent discussions of policy can be found in David Farber, ed., *The Sixties: From Memory to History* (Chapel Hill, 1994), and Margaret Weir, Ann Orloff, and Theda Skocpol, eds., *The Politics of Social Policy in the United States* (Princeton, 1988).

1. FROM CIVIL RIGHTS TO RACE

There is an enormous and powerful literature on civil rights and race in the United States during the 1960s. Three of the many fine local studies are Sidney Fine, *Violence in the Model*

City: The Cavanagh Administration, Race Relations, and the Detroit Riot of 1967 (Ann Arbor, 1989); John Dittmer, *Local People: The Struggle for Civil Rights in Mississippi* (Urbana, Ill., 1994); and Charles Payne, *I've Got the Light of Freedom: The Organizing Tradition and the Mississippi Freedom Struggle* (Berkeley, 1995). Superb overviews of national policy may be found in Hugh Davis Graham, *The Civil Rights Era: Origins and Development of National Policy, 1960–1972* (New York, 1990), and in Mark Stern, *Calculating Visions: Kennedy, Johnson, and Civil Rights* (New Brunswick, N.J., 1992). For Northern activities, see James Ralph, Jr., *Northern Protest: Martin Luther King, Jr., Chicago, and the Civil Rights Movement* (Cambridge, Mass., 1993).

Several studies were particularly useful for the urban riots and national legislation. In particular see James Button, *Black Violence: Political Impact of the 1960s Riots* (Princeton, 1978), and Gerald Horne, *Fire This Time: The Watts Uprising and the 1960s* (Charlottesville, Va., 1995) for the riots. On legislation, see Michael Brown and Steven Erie, "Blacks and the Legacy of the Great Society: The Economic and Political Impact of Federal Social Policy," *Public Policy* 29 (Summer 1981), 299–330; Stephen Halpern, *On the Limits of the Law: The Ironic Legacy of Title VI of the 1964 Civil Rights Act* (Baltimore, 1995); Bernard Schwartz, ed., *Statutory History of the United States: Civil Rights, Part II* (New York, 1970); and Charles and Barbara Whalen, *The Longest Debate: A Legislative History of the 1964 Civil Rights Act* (Cabin John, Md., 1985). One of the most controversial reports of these years is analyzed in Lee Rainwater and William L. Yancey, *The Moynihan Report and the Politics of Controversy* (Cambridge, Mass., 1967). For a look back at the impact of these events, see Thomas and Mary Edsall, *Chain Reaction: The Impact of Race, Rights, and Taxes on American Politics* (New York, 1991).

2. THE WAR ON POVERTY

The historical debate over the War on Poverty has frequently been as contentious as the legislative debate was thirty years ago. Michael Gillette has compiled a selection of oral histories in *Launching the War on Poverty: An Oral History* (New York, 1996). Commentary from conservatives, which itself became an issue, can be found in Charles Murray, *Losing Ground: American Social Policy, 1950–1980* (New York, 1984). Analysis from two policy architects may be found in Frances Fox Piven and Richard Cloward, *Regulating the Poor: The Functions of Public Welfare* (New York, 1971). More recent, and more balanced, assessments can be found in Martha Davis, *Brutal Need: Lawyers and the Welfare Rights Movement, 1960–1973* (New Haven, 1993); Nicholas Lemann, *The Promised Land: The Great Black Migration and How It Changed America* (New York, 1991); James Patterson, *America's Struggle Against Poverty, 1900–1994* (Cambridge, Mass., 1994); Jill Quadagno, *The Color of Welfare: How Racism Undermined the War on Poverty* (New York, 1994); and William Julius Wilson, *The Truly Disadvantaged: The Inner City, the Underclass, and Public Policy* (Chicago, 1987). In addition, two works by Michael Katz remain among the most important investigations of this issue: *The "Underclass" Debate: Views from History* (Princeton, 1993), and *The Undeserving Poor: From the War on Poverty to the War on Welfare* (New York, 1989).

Several older studies that document changes wrought by federal policies remain useful. See in particular Robert Haveman, ed., *A Decade of Federal Antipoverty Programs: Achievements, Failures, and Lessons* (New York, 1977); Robert Haveman, *Poverty Policy and Poverty Research: The Great Society and the Social Sciences* (Madison, Wisc., 1987); Louise Lander, ed., *War on Poverty* (New York, 1967); and Sar Levitan, *The Great Society's Poor Law: A New Approach to Poverty* (Baltimore, 1969).

For a look beyond the Johnson years, see Edward Berkowitz, *America's Welfare State: From Roosevelt to Reagan* (Baltimore,

1991); Phoebe Cottingham and David Ellwood, eds., *Welfare Policy for the 1990s* (Cambridge, Mass., 1989); Burton Kaufman, *The Presidency of James Earl Carter, Jr.* (Lawrence, Kans., 1993); and A. James Reichley, *Conservatives in an Age of Change: The Nixon and Ford Administrations* (Washington, D.C., 1981).

3. HEALTH AND EDUCATION

Medicare, and health reform in general, remains a complex and often misunderstood subject. Helpful in charting my way through the policy maze were Edward Berkowitz, *Mr. Social Security: The Life of Wilbur J. Cohen* (Lawrence, Kans., 1995), and Theodore Marmor, *The Politics of Medicare* (Chicago, 1973). Also see Teresa Coughlin, Leighton Ku, and John Holahan, *Medicaid Since 1980: Costs, Coverage, and the Shifting Alliance Between the Federal Government and the States* (Washington, D.C., 1994); Theodore Marmor, Jerry Mashaw, and Philip Harvey, *America's Misunderstood Welfare State: Persistent Myths, Enduring Realities* (New York, 1990); Marilyn Moon, *Medicare Now and in the Future* (Washington, D.C., 1993); and Robert and Rosemary Stevens, *Welfare Medicine in America: A Case Study of Medicaid* (New York, 1974).

Education, while a bit easier to understand, is no less complex or controversial. Important for an overview is Hugh Davis Graham, *The Uncertain Triumph: Federal Education Policy in the Kennedy and Johnson Years* (Chapel Hill, 1984). Political issues are also covered in Philip Meranto, *The Politics of Federal Aid to Education in 1965* (Syracuse, 1967), and Diane Ravitch, *The Trouble Crusade: American Education, 1945–1980* (New York, 1983). Important specialized studies are Stephen Bailey and Edith Mosher, *ESEA: The Office of Education Administers a Law* (Syracuse, 1968); Julie Roy Jeffrey, *Education for Children of the Poor: A Study of the Origins and Implementation of the Elementary and Secondary Education Act of 1965* (Columbus, Ohio, 1978); and Edward Zigler and Susan Muenchow, *Head Start: The Inside Story of America's Most Successful Educational Experiment* (New York, 1992).

4. MODEL CITIES

The two most useful studies for my purposes were Bernard Frieden and Marshall Kaplan, *The Politics of Neglect: Urban Aid from Model Cities to Revenue Sharing* (Cambridge, Mass., 1975), and Charles Haar, *Between the Idea and the Reality: A Study in the Origin, Fate, and Legacy of the Model Cities Program* (Boston, 1975). For a conservative view, see Edward Banfield, "Making a New Federal Program: Model Cities, 1964–1968," in Walter Williams and Richard Elmore, eds., *Social Program Implementation* (New York, 1976), pp. 183–218, as well as Banfield's *The Unheavenly City: The Nature and Future of Our Urban Crisis* (Boston, 1968). Two other studies of importance are George Smerk, *The Federal Role in Urban Mass Transportation* (Bloomington, Ind., 1991), and Robert Wood, "Model Cities: What Went Wrong— the Program or Its Critics?" in Naomi Carmon, ed., *Neighbourhood Policy and Programmes: Past and Present* (New York, 1990), pp. 61–73. Two recent works that contribute important new historical evidence to our analysis of the urban crisis are Robert Halpern, *Rebuilding the Inner City: A History of Neighborhood Initiatives to Address Poverty in the United States* (New York, 1995), and Thomas Sugrue, *The Origins of the Urban Crisis: Race and Inequality in Postwar Detroit* (Princeton, 1996).

5. QUALITY OF LIFE

A synthetic overview of this issue remains to be written. Among the specialized studies that proved useful were Lewis L. Gould, *Lady Bird Johnson and the Environment* (Lawrence, Kans., 1988); Robert Mayer, *The Consumer Movement: Guardians of the*

Marketplace (Boston, 1989); Mark Nadel, *The Politics of Consumer Protection* (Indianapolis, 1971); Michael Pertschuk, *Revolt Against Regulation: The Rise and Pause of the Consumer Movement* (Berkeley, 1982); and David Vogel, *Fluctuating Fortunes: The Political Power of Business in America* (New York, 1989). For the growing concern about crime, see *The Challenge of Crime in a Free Society: A Report by the President's Commission on Law Enforcement and the Administration of Justice* (Washington, D.C., 1967), and *The Challenge of Crime in a Free Society: Perspectives on the Report of the President's Commission on Law Enforcement and the Administration of Justice* (New York, 1971).

6. Assessing the Great Society

There are almost as many judgments on the Great Society as there are politicians, historians, and political scientists. For criticism from the left, see Richard Flacks, "Is the Great Society Just a Barbecue?" *New Republic* (January 29, 1966), 18–19, 22–23; Marvin Gettleman and David Mermelstein, eds., *The Great Society Reader: The Failure of American Liberalism* (New York, 1967); and Ira Katznelson, "Was the Great Society a Lost Opportunity?" in Steve Fraser and Gary Gerstle, eds., *The Rise and Fall of the New Deal Order, 1930–1980* (Princeton, 1989). A Republican view is in the Republican Party Coordinating Committee's *Choice for America* (n.p., 1968).

For other illuminating assessments, see Henry J. Aaron, *Politics and the Professors: The Great Society in Perspective* (Washington, D.C., 1978); Doris Kearns, *Lyndon Johnson and the American Dream* (New York, 1976); Mel Grinspan, ed., *The Great Society Revisited: Success, Failure, or Remorse?* (Memphis, 1993); Sar Levitan and Robert Taggart, "The Great Society Did Succeed," *Political Science Quarterly* 91 (Winter 1976–1977), 601–618; Levitan and Taggart, *The Promise of Greatness* (Cambridge, Mass., 1976); and John Schwartz, *America's Hidden Success: A Reassessment of Twenty Years of Public Policy* (New York, 1983). Two fairly recent studies that draw together a variety of interpretive essays are Barbara Jordan and Elspeth Rostow, eds., *The Great Society: A Twenty Year Critique* (Austin, Tex., 1986), and Marshall Kaplan and Peggy Cuciti, eds., *The Great Society and Its Legacy* (Durham, N.C., 1986).

Index

Affirmative action, 43–44, 52, 55, 152–153
Aid to Families with Dependent Children (AFDC), 61–62, 108, 112, 190
Alinsky, Saul, 73
American Medical Association (AMA), 95, 96, 98, 99, 101, 109, 191
Appalachian Aid Bill (1965), 72, 91

Baby boom, 17, 115
Beatles, 6
Beautification, 172–173
Boone, Richard, 68
Brown case (1954), 24, 122
Buckley, William F., Jr., 18, 164
Byrnes, John, 99, 100

Califano, Joseph, 13, 16
Carmichael, Stokely, 42–43, 48
Carter, Jimmy, 188, 189, 192
Cavanagh, Jerome, 66, 140, 147
Celebrezze, Anthony, 117–118
Child Development Group of Mississippi (CDGM), 77–78
Civil rights, 23–55, 184, 186
Civil Rights Act (1960), 37
Civil Rights Act (1964), 23, 25, 28–31, 35, 36, 47–48, 54, 71, 122–123, 153, 185, 186

Civil Rights Act (1966), 50–51
Clinton, Bill, 186, 190, 193
Cohen, Wilbur, 102–103, 104–105, 106, 117
Coleman Report (1966), 82, 124–125
Community Action Program (CAP), 8, 65, 68–69, 73, 132, 146, 187; and Community Action Agencies (CAAs), 68, 187
Congress of Racial Equality (CORE), 40, 42, 81
Connor, Eugene "Bull," 25
Consumer legislation, 163–172, 182
Crime, 180–182. *See also* Detroit riot; Watts riot.
Cultural life, 177–180
Culture of poverty theory, 58

Daley, Richard, J., 49, 66, 73, 123
Demonstration Cities and Metropolitan Redevelopment Act (1966), 138–139, 140–145
Department of Housing and Urban Development (HUD), 135, 137, 144–145, 147, 150–151, 197
Detroit riot (1967), 147–149
Dirksen, Everett, 26, 28, 50, 53, 128, 145

Eastland, James, 27, 37–38, 78
Economic Opportunity Act
    (1964), 64–72, 132
Economic Research and Action
    Project (ERAP), 69
Education, 114–130; parochial
    school issue, 115–117
Eisenhower, Dwight: and
    modern Republicanism, 18
Election of 1964, 19–21, 30
Elementary and Secondary
    Education Act (1965),
    117–128, 130; 1967
    amendments, 128–129
Environmental regulation,
    173–177, 194; pollution,
    173–176; wilderness
    protection, 176–177
Equal Employment Opportunity
    Commission (EEOC), 26, 29,
    30, 52
Ervin, Sam, 27, 38

Fair housing, 52–54
Fino, Paul, 142–143
Freedom Rides, 29
Freedom Summer (1964), 32

Gans, Herbert, 134–135
Gardner, John, 103–104, 108,
    117, 128, 199
Gingrich, Newt, 3, 5, 185
Goldwater, Barry, 18, 19, 21,
    31–32, 33, 69
Gonzalez, Henry B., 134, 143
Goodell, Charles, 79, 118
Goodwin, Richard, 11, 163,
    195–196
Green, Edith, 74, 81, 121, 128

Hackett, David, 68
Hamer, Fannie Lou, 33, 40
Harris, Fred, 110, 151–152
Hayden, Tom, 69
Head Start, 76–78
Heller, Walter, 56, 64
Higher Education Act (1965),
    120–121, 126–127; 1968
    amendments, 130
Housing Act of 1964, 133
Housing and Urban
    Development Act (1965),
    133–135; (1968), 153–156, 157
Humphrey, Hubert, 26, 27–28,
    31, 33, 78

Javits, Jacob, 27, 38
Job Corps, 64–65, 74, 79
John Birch Society, 31, 62
Johnson, Lady Bird, 163, 173
Johnson, Lyndon, 3, 5, 6, 8, 11,
    50–51, 147, 168–169; concept
    of consensus, 18; Howard
    University Speech (1965),
    43–44, 45; personality of, 9–10;
    and poverty, 63–64, 65; use of
    task forces, 16–17, 136,
    158–159; visions of Great
    Society, 10–16, 20, 22, 56, 72,
    95, 97, 101, 114–115, 125, 137,
    163, 172–173, 195

Katzenbach, Nicholas, 34, 38,
    138–139
Kennedy, Edward, 120
Kennedy, John F., 5, 8, 18, 23, 83;
    legislative program, 5–6,
    14–15, 56, 72, 116, 133
Kennedy, Robert, 66, 110, 120,
    139

Keppel, Francis, 117, 123
Kerner Commission, 47, 53, 92, 149, 151–152
Kerr-Mills Bill (1960), 96, 100
King-Anderson Bill, 97–100. *See also* Medicare.
King, Martin Luther, Jr., 34, 36, 48, 49–50, 54, 145

Legal Services Program, 74–75, 187
Lewis, John, 24–25
Lindsay, John, 75–76, 139–140
Long, Russell, 27, 109, 110
Losing Ground (Murray), 88–89

Managerial liberalism, 9, 15
March on Washington (1963), 24, 25, 59, 92
McCone, John, 46–47
McNamara, Robert, 66, 82
Medicaid, 92, 100, 103–104, 106–109, 111–114, 192
Medicare, 92, 95–114, 191–193, 197
Meredith, James, 48
Mills, Wilbur, 15, 96, 100, 109, 110
Mississippi Freedom Democratic Party (MFDP), 32–33, 78
Mitchell, Joseph, 62–63
Model Cities, 131–162; urban renewal, 134–136, 157–158. *See also* Demonstration Cities and Metropolitan Redevelopment Act.
Moyers, Bill, 10, 16, 31
Moynihan, Daniel Patrick, 44–45, 46, 58–59, 90, 165, 189
Muskie, Edmund, 27, 141, 174

Nader, Ralph, 164–167
National Association for the Advancement of Colored People (NAACP), 40, 45, 81
National Defense Education Act (1958), 115
National Welfare Rights Organization (NWRO), 86, 109
Newark (N.J.) Community Union Project (NCUP), 69
Nixon, Richard, 18, 93, 157, 188–189, 196

Office of Economic Opportunity (OEO), 58, 65, 70, 72–73, 76–84
Ohlin, Lloyd, 75, 198
Operation Dixie, 34
The Other America (Harrington), 58, 61

Peterson, Esther, 164, 169
Philadelphia Plan, 55, 152–153
Phillips, Howard, 57–58
Poverty, theories of, 58–61

Quie, Albert, 79, 127

Reagan, Ronald, 51, 79, 90, 107, 145, 158, 189–190, 192
Republican Coordinating Committee, 156–157
Ribicoff, Abraham, 138, 139
Russell, Richard, 26, 27

Safe Streets and Crime Control
Act (1967), 151
Selma, Ala., 34–35
Shriver, Sargent, 74, 78, 81, 83
Silent Spring (Carson), 172
Sixties: idealism of, 6, 57, 93, 198;
in historical memory, 3
Smith, Howard, 118–119
Social Security Amendments
(1967), 107–112
Southern Christian Leadership
Conference (SCLC), 34–35,
49–50, 81
Stennis, John, 27, 77–78
Student Non-Violent
Coordinating Committee
(SNCC), 7, 40, 42, 69, 81
Students for a Democratic
Society (SDS), 7, 69, 86

Taft, Robert, Jr., 19, 67
Tax cut (1964), 14–15, 63, 85
Thurmond, Strom, 28, 41
Tower, John, 27, 33–34, 69, 98,
141, 174

Vietnam War, 7, 9, 14, 15, 17, 48,
54, 81, 83, 87, 114, 146, 196
Voting Rights Bill (1965), 34–42,
47–48, 54, 60, 185, 197

Wallace, George, 28–29, 41, 79,
123–124
Wallace, Lurleen, 51, 79
War on Poverty, 34, 56–94;
debates over, 86–94, 96
Watts riot (1965), 42, 45–48, 85,
149
Weaver, Robert, 138, 142
Wiley, George, 85–86
Willis, Dr. Benjamin, 119–120
Wilson, William Julius, 89–92,
161–162, 193–194
Wirtz, Willard, 66, 71
Women's movement, 7, 29
Wood, Robert, 135, 158–159, 161

Yarmolinsky, Adam, 71
Young Americans for Freedom,
7, 58, 62

A NOTE ON THE AUTHOR

John A. Andrew III is professor of history at Franklin &
Marshall College. Born in Boston, Massachusetts, he studied at the University of New Hampshire and the University of Texas at Austin. His research interests have focused
on movements for social and political change in American
history. Mr. Andrew's other books are *The Other Side of the
Sixties, From Revivals to Removal,* and *Rebuilding the Christian Commonwealth.*

BOOKS IN THE AMERICAN WAYS SERIES

William Earl Weeks, *Building the Continental Empire: American Expansion from the Revolution to the Civil War*

Jean V. Matthews, *Women's Struggle for Equality: The First Phase, 1820–1876*

Curtis D. Johnson, *Redeeming America: Evangelicals and the Road to Civil War*

J. Matthew Gallman, *The North Fights the Civil War: The Home Front*

Maury Klein, *The Flowering of the Third America: The Making of an Organizational Society, 1850–1920*

Larry M. Logue, *To Appomattox and Beyond: The Civil War Soldier in War and Peace*

Robert Muccigrosso, *Celebrating the New World: Chicago's Columbian Exposition of 1893*

Daniel Nelson, *Shifting Fortunes: The Rise and Decline of American Labor, from the 1820s to the Present*

Thomas R. Pegram, *Battling Demon Rum: The Struggle for a Dry America, 1800–1933*

Roger Daniels, *Not Like Us: Immigrants and Minorities in America, 1890–1924*

Burton W. Peretti, *Jazz in American Culture*

Iwan W. Morgan, *Deficit Government: Taxing and Spending in Modern America*

D. Clayton James and Anne Sharp Wells, *From Pearl Harbor to V-J Day: The American Armed Forces in World War II*

John W. Jeffries, *Wartime America: The World War II Home Front*

John Earl Haynes, *Red Scare or Red Menace?: American Communism and Anticommunism in the Cold War Era*

Mark J. White, *Missiles in Cuba: Kennedy, Khrushchev, Castro and the 1962 Crisis*

John A. Salmond, *"My Mind Set on Freedom": A History of the Civil Rights Movement, 1954–1968*

John A. Andrew III, *Lyndon Johnson and the Great Society*

Lewis L. Gould, *1968: The Election That Changed America*